There Is Fire
In The Blood

Rev Kathryn L. Smith

PUBLISHED by PARABLE
Earthly Stories with a Heavenly Meaning

There Is Fire In The Blood
Rev. Kathryn L. Smith

Copyright © Kathryn L. Smith
November, 2016

Published By Parables
October, 2016

All Rights Reserved. No part of this book may be reproduced or utilized in any form or by any means, electronic or mechanical, including photocopying, recording, or by any information storage and retrieval system, without permission in writing from the author.

Unless otherwise specified Scripture quotations are taken from the authorized version of the King James Bible.

ISBN 978-1-945698-08-8
Printed in the United States of America

Readers should be aware that Internet Web sites offered as citations and/or sources for further information may have been changed or disappeared between the time this was written and when it is read.

There Is Fire
In The Blood

Rev Kathryn L. Smith

PUBLISHED by PARABLES
Earthly Stories with a Heavenly Meaning

Acknowledgements

Thank you to my wonderful husband, William R. Smith II, [Buzz] who loved me all these years and allowed me to follow God's call, even when it meant I was gone preaching or consumed with writing.

I deeply appreciate all those who made me the woman of faith, the minister and the author that I am. I want to especially thank my Pastor Timothy A. Naylor, and those previous Pastors who have encouraged and instructed me over the years. I want to mention Pastor Rick Naylor, Pastor Mark Maynard, and Pastor Sherman J. Smith III; these men of faith invested in my spiritual growth and served as shepherds to my soul. I also want to honor the men and women whose ministries and books have shaped my faith; some of those names have faded over time, but their truths have become ingrained within my spirit; to all those who taught me but were not specifically cited in this book—thank you.

Mostly, I want to thank the Lord Jesus Christ who loved me when I was lost, called me when I was nothing and anointed me to do his work. I pray that He will be glorified and lifted high in all I have attempted for him.

Table Of Contents

Fire in the Blood—Foundational Truth	11
First things First—In the Beginning	15
Cain and Abel Offerings	23
Walking in the Blood	29
God Provides His Own Lamb	35
From Passover to Passing Over	39
Consecration and Dedications	45
God's Fire When the Wood is Wet	53
Holy Blood on the Altar of the Cross	61
Identification Is Our Response	69
Pentecost	79
She Put the Blood First—A Testimony of the Miraculous	83
The Blood is Enough	87
Works Cited	93

Leviticus 17:11 (KJV) *11 For the life of the flesh is in the blood: and I have given it to you upon the altar to make an atonement for your souls: for it is the blood that maketh an atonement for the soul.*

Fire In The Blood - Foundational Truth

Every time the blood was shed it was a foretaste of the blood of Jesus. The blood offering and the resulting fire were deeply intertwined to produce the plan of God for mankind. It is the life of Jesus in the blood that gives us access to the fire of the Holy Spirit even now.

It was holy fire that consumed the sacrifices of Abel, Aaron and Elijah. After Passover there was a column of fire that led the children of Israel through the wilderness. A flame of fire shone above the Mercy Seat on the Ark of the Covenant. The Cross produced a manifestation of fire in the upper room at Pentecost. Fire fell symbolically throughout the Bible. In every case it was the same fire and the same Holy Spirit that came to bring the promise. These miraculous and powerful demonstrations were a part of God's divine purpose. **Supernatural fire always fell in response to the blood.**

Leviticus 17:11 (KJV) 11 *For the life of the flesh is in the blood: and I have given it to you upon the altar to make an atonement for your souls: for it is the blood that maketh an atonement for the soul.* God gave His life-producing blood to provide us with access into his presence, to restore and to redeem man. No move of the miraculous and powerful comes before an acknowledgement of the sacrifice. Today we look to the saving blood of Jesus. There was a time when God honored the blood of a lamb as a substitute—an atonement. That was a temporary state of limited grace. [Heb. 10:1-10] But now the blood of the Son of God has been shed and that blood can and does produce power just as it did at Pentecost. **If we want the fire to fall we have to go by way of the blood.**

Christ was slain from the foundation of the earth, [Rev. 13:8] which is only possible in the realm of the eternal. Time is an earthly concept. Linear time is only present in this world. God, who is eternal, lives in the eternal. There is a perpetual now in heaven where past, present and future unite as one. It is as if time were a circle and God sits over the whole of the circle. It is difficult for us to think this way because to us there is a very definite yesterday, today, and tomorrow, but in many primitive cultures the people had no concept of time and no words to describe when something occurred. Very small children have no understanding of time. As my mother progressed through Alzheimer's, she lost her ability to differentiate time; this morning or last week or three years ago all became the same to her. She could not follow a calendar with blank squares before the first day of the month. God alone knows and sees all of time in its proper prospective. **Isaiah 46:9-10 (KJV)** *9 Remember the former things of old: for I am God, and there is none else; I am God, and there is none like me, 10 Declaring the end from the beginning, and from ancient times the things that are not yet done, saying, My counsel shall stand, and I will do all my pleasure:* [See also Psalms 90:2 and Rev. 21:6]

In Paul's letter to the Ephesians we catch another glimpse of the plan and purpose of God at work in the blood sacrifice to bring mankind into his presence once more. **Ephesians 1:3-10 (MSG)** *3 How blessed is God! And what a blessing he is! He's the Father of our Master, Jesus Christ, and takes us to the high places of blessing in him. 4 Long before he laid down earth's foundations, he had us in mind, had settled on us as the focus of his love, to be made whole and holy by his love. 5 Long, long ago he decided to adopt us into his family through Jesus Christ. (What pleasure he took in planning this!) 6 He wanted us to enter into the celebration of his lavish* *gift-giving by the hand of his beloved Son. 7 Because of the sacrifice of the Messiah, his blood poured out on the altar of the Cross, we're a free people— free of penalties and punishments chalked up by all our misdeeds. And not just barely free, either. Abundantly free! 8 He thought of everything, provided for everything we could possibly need, 9 letting us in on the plans he took such delight in making. He set it all out before us in Christ, 10 a long-range plan in which everything would be brought together and summed up in him, everything in deepest heaven, everything on planet earth.*

If we could grasp the fullness of the reality of time as God knows it, we could find a resurrected Christ in the manger and a defeated devil tempting Him in the wilderness. We could be present at the cross and the resurrection. We could have an awareness of the blood flowing over us and setting us free. Experience is bound by time only on the earth, and all that God intended for us to have as a result of the shed blood and resurrection was a finished work in the heart of God before Adam sinned.

That finished work of redemption is beautifully portrayed in the book of Jeremiah. **Jeremiah 18:3-6 (KJV)** *3 Then I went down to the potter's house, and, behold, he wrought a work on the wheels. 4 And the vessel that he made of clay was marred in the hand of the potter: so he made it again another vessel, as seemed good to the potter to make it. 5 Then the word of the LORD came to me, saying, 6 O house of Israel, cannot I do with you as this potter? saith the LORD. Behold, as the clay is in the potter's hand, so are ye in mine hand, O house of Israel.* The vessel was marred while still in the hands of the potter. Adam was molded from the clay, just as the pots were in the days of Jeremiah. There in the Garden man became flawed; mankind was fallen. Adam was much less than the image of God he was created to be. So God made him again, another. God, through the cross and the spilled blood of his own Son, not only redeemed fallen man, but remade him.

In his second letter to the church at Corinth, Paul wrote of the remaking of mankind. **II Corinthians 5:17 (KJV)** *17 Therefore if any man be in Christ, he is a new creature: old things are passed away; behold, all things are become new.* God took the man who was living and breathing in this realm, man who was subject to death because of the fall and remade him into a new species. The redeemed were born again, men with the very life of God inside. They had been separated by sin from the God who loved them, but through the blood God brought man back into fellowship. Adam did not see all of that when he fell. Redemption was not a finished work in the earth realm of time and space, but it was already accepted in the court of heaven.

I worked for twenty five years as a sign language interpreter for the deaf, and I still interpret at church when hearing impaired people come. I was signing and singing at home the other day when I noticed something in my reflection. When I signed the word glory I saw that it looked like I was dipping my finger into the nail print that is assumed to be in the lower palm when signing the word Jesus. The touch finger reaching into the palm, <u>into the blood of Jesus, produces the shining glory of God</u>. It came as a revelation that once you have touched the blood, you can experience the glory. It was part of the inspiration for this teaching.

Blood always precedes forgiveness, deliverance and great anointing. In this study we will look at how the blood and fire fell, in the sacrifices of men like Abel, Abraham, Moses, Elijah and of course, Jesus. In every case blood shed produced a powerful manifestation. **It is the same fire that fell, the same Holy Ghost who moved then and continues to move today. We want to honor the blood and see the fire fall!**

First Things First - In The Beginning

In the beginning of our time, when the earth was new and God created Adam, He made him like himself. The triune God was speaking and said, *"Let us create man in our image."* The fullness of the trinity agreed to make man as a totally new order of being. He was not animal, not Angel, but a separate creation. He, like the Godhead, was a triune being. Man was spirit, soul and body.

Genesis 1:26-27 (KJV) *26 And God said, Let us make man in our image, after our likeness: and let them have dominion over the fish of the sea, and over the fowl of the air, and over the cattle, and over all the earth, and over every creeping thing that creepeth upon the earth. 27 So God created man in his own image, in the image of God created he him; male and female created he them.*

If man was indeed the expression of God on the earth, the very image of Him, then what did God look like? What attributes did he have? According to the Strong's Concordance that word image is the Hebrew word #6754 *tselem* which means an outline, shadow, or resemblance. That would imply that we have physical attributes like God.

Genesis 2: 7 (KJV) *7 And the LORD God formed man of the dust of the ground, and breathed into his nostrils the breath of life; and man became a living soul.* According to the original language, Adam was handmade, squeezed into shape. God molded him; He placed his hands all over the external shell of man. Then God took life from within him, and breathed it into Adam. The man had God-life inside him, he became a living spirit. He was made to be like his creator, an eternal spirit, with a soul that could freely think and speak. Man would also have a body with God-created blood flowing through it.

We know a little of what the Bible says God looks like. Among those glimpses into the glory we see the words fire, and light repeated. **Deuteronomy 4: 24 (KJV)** *24 For the LORD thy God is a consuming fire.*

Habakkuk 3:3-4 (KJV) *3 God came from Teman, and the Holy One from mount Paran. Selah. <u>His glory covered the heavens, and the earth was full of his praise. 4 And his brightness was as the light; he had horns coming out of his hand: and there was the hiding of his power.</u>* God was shining with light, and fiery in appearance with lightning like power, coming out of his hands. That is a picture that could inspire the image of a superhero.

Ezekiel 1:26-28 (KJV) *26 And above the firmament that was over their heads was the likeness of a throne, as the appearance of a sapphire stone: and upon the likeness of the throne was the likeness as the appearance of a man above upon it. 27 And I saw as the colour of amber, as the appearance of fire round about within it, from the appearance of his loins even upward, and from the appearance of his loins even downward, I saw as it were the appearance of fire, and it had brightness round about. 28 As the appearance of the bow that is in the cloud in the day of rain, so was the appearance of the brightness round about. This was the appearance of the likeness of the glory of the LORD. And when I saw it, I fell upon my face...* That is another picture of the Lord covered by or made of fire; Ezekiel said it was the likeness of His glory.

We find a reference in the New Testament as well. There came a time when the disciples saw a glimpse into the glory as Jesus was transfigured into something more like the image of God we have seen described in scripture. **Luke 9:28-29 (KJV)** *28 And it came to pass about an eight days after these sayings, he took Peter and John and James, and went up into a mountain to pray. 29 And as he prayed, the fashion of his countenance was altered, and his raiment was white and glistering.* That image of him was repeated when John saw him from the Isle of Patmos. **Revelation 1:16 (KJV)** *16 And he had in his right hand seven stars: and out of his mouth went a sharp twoedged sword: and his countenance was as the sun shineth in his strength.*

The author of James called him *"the Father of lights, with whom is no variableness, neither shadow of turning."* (**James 1:17 KJV**) We are told in (**1 Timothy 6:16 KJV**) that *"He dwells in unapproachable light."* As we look for other references of God we see Him repeatedly covered with a cloud of fire and glory. If Adam was like him, then he too was clothed with the fiery glory.

Psalm 8:3-8 (KJV) *3 When I consider thy heavens, the work of thy fingers, the moon and the stars, which thou hast ordained; 4 What is man, that thou art mindful of him? and the son of man, that thou visitest him? 5 For thou hast made him a little lower than the angels, [**Elohim**] and hast crowned [**atar**] him with glory [**kabod**] and honour. 6 Thou madest him to have dominion over the works of thy hands; thou hast put all things under his feet: 7 All sheep and oxen, yea, and the beasts of the field; 8 The fowl of the air, and the fish of the sea, and whatsoever passeth through the paths of the seas.*

There is truth bound to the definition of those three words in the original language. First, look at the word that was translated as angels, it is *Elohim:* Strong's Hebrew word #430 which is usually translated as the plural form of the word God, and rarely as angels. Crowned is Strong's Hebrew word #5849 *atar* meaning to encircle or compass or crown. Glory in verse 5 was Strong's Hebrew word #3519 *kabod* which means weighty, splendor and glorious honor. With these three definitions in mind we can see that the Psalmist was speaking of the position of mankind as just below the Godhead. Man was covered with and encircled by the weighty presence and glory of God and reigning over all of creation. That can only be man as he was before the fall. That is the picture of Adam covered in the glory and living as God created him.

Adam and Eve lived for an unknown period of time in perfect fellowship with their Creator. He gave them all they needed, and fellowshipped with them daily. They had dominion over the whole of creation. God gave them total provision in a perfect world, and only one restriction. **Genesis 2:16-17 (KJV)** *16 And the LORD God commanded the man, saying, Of every tree of the garden thou mayest freely eat: 17 But of the tree of the knowledge of good and evil, thou shalt not eat of it: for in the day that thou eatest thereof thou shalt surely die.*

Over the course of time, they failed; more accurately stated, they openly rebelled. "To rebel in an act of disobedience that declared independence from Him was to disconnect with the source of life and plunge into death." (Smith p.27) They had not broken some manmade law or an arbitrary rule of conduct, they had refused God as Lord, and they had turned away from union with him. They had said we choose our own way. Their disobedience must be judged. The sin was not limited to them, but affected all of the generations of men yet to be born on the earth. Since every man would come from the seed still within Adam, that damaged image and sin-tainted seed would plummet all of mankind into spiritual death.

Genesis 3:1-7 (KJV) *1 Now the serpent was more subtil than any beast of the field which the LORD God had made. And he said unto the woman, Yea, hath God said, Ye shall not eat of every tree of the garden? 2 And the woman said unto the serpent, We may eat of the fruit of the trees of the garden: 3 But of the fruit of the tree which is in the midst of the garden, God hath said, Ye shall not eat of it, neither shall ye touch it, lest ye die. 4 And the serpent said unto the woman, Ye shall not surely die: 5 For God doth know that in the day ye eat thereof, then your eyes shall be opened, and ye shall be as gods, knowing good and evil. 6 And when the woman saw that the tree was good for food, and that it was pleasant to the eyes, and a tree to be desired to make one wise, she took of the fruit thereof, and did eat, and gave also unto her husband with her; and he did eat. 7 And the eyes of them both were opened, and they knew that they were naked; and they sewed fig leaves together, and made themselves aprons.*

God could not ignore their sin, He had to find a way to cover over the failure of man and his rebellion until a true redemption through the blood of Jesus could be made. "Apart from causing creation to cease, there was nothing God could do to suspend the results of their sin." (Smith p.27) That day death came to their relationship with God; they were living only in the flesh. **Romans 6:23 (KJV)** *23 For the wages of sin is death; but the gift of God is eternal life through Jesus Christ our Lord.*

When Adam sinned, he realized the glory was gone; the flame had gone out. He no longer looked like God. Man was indeed naked and ashamed and he no longer came running to God. Adam's sin separated God from the ones He loved. In both his heart and his body, Adam was no longer God's reflection on earth.

Adam and Eve did not seek God and beg forgiveness; there is no record that they repented. Instead they made aprons of leaves to hide their nakedness. Fig leaves may have made man less embarrassed, but they were never enough to hide their spiritual condition or cover the root problem which was sin. Only blood could delay judgment. It was God, not they, who made the first move toward restoration. "The first response of God to the sin of man was to give them the gift of animal sacrifice, in which the sacred lifeblood of the animal was shed in death, being poured out on behalf of the sinner under the penalty of death." (Smith p. 101)

God made that first blood sacrifice. In order to purchase grace as a covering atonement for Adam and Eve, a life was taken. For the first time blood was spilled. It should have been Adam who died, but the price of all mankind was too high, so God chose for an animal to die. Judgment was postponed but the damage was done. An animal became a substitute so that man could live a while longer. God had a bigger plan, to do more than offer an animal. Jesus would taste of death so man might live. God's own blood must be shed.

Adam must have been devastated to see the result of his sin. He had been a reflection of God, covered in the glory, but now he was covered in the bloody skin of a sacrifice. He knew the cost of his personal sin when he saw an animal die to cover him. Adam knew that it was only a temporary covering; it was not a restoration of the glory.

Those skins merely covered his nakedness—they did not take away the impurity of his heart. That blood was the first that was shed on earth to represent the true blood of redemption. Think not only of that stinking, bloody, dead skin, covering the flesh of man, but also the flesh of man that had been covering an eternal spirit that was intended to live in perfect fellowship with God. Made in God's image, mankind was never intended to die. Sin marred the clay the Master Craftsman had molded and the true remedy was already in place within the heart of God. "Man's body—an earthen vessel—could be broken and the blood poured out, a life for a life. If a Divine One would go to earth Incarnate and live without sin in a body prepared, His vessel could be broken and His perfect Life poured out in His Blood for the remission of all sin." (Brim, p. 50)

Adam was lost. He was spiritually dead. Unity with his Creator was missing. The glory and presence of God within him had vanished; the infusion of righteousness that let the Eternal God fellowship with Adam was destroyed. The fire and the glory were gone, and the relationship between God and man was horribly broken. Sin separated them. Adam's rebellion took some of the essence of God from inside and left a hole in the heart of man that only that presence could fill. God was making a plan to redeem all of what Adam lost. God's plan was to make man again, anew, another. Just like the potter in Jeremiah 18:1-6. I do not know why the plan had to take so many years. I do know that God had to legally get Jesus to earth. Since Adam was the ruler of this realm, when he fell the earth was changed. The lease on planet earth had been turned over to Satan, meaning the clay was no longer clean and useful. It was tainted by sin. No new body could be formed from the ground. The essence of every man was still inside Adam's fallen body; no human born on the earth in the natural would ever be able to restore the glory.

Sin demanded the shedding of blood that brought grace, and eventually real forgiveness and real life; it has always been about the blood. Everything about the covenant of blood comes from and ends in heaven. Jesus became a man and shed his blood here, but it was planned and accepted in heaven in order to minister to man before the world was created. Rev 13:8 called Jesus the *Lamb slain from the foundation of the earth.*

THERE IS FIRE IN THE BLOOD

Where was the fire in response to the blood that first time it was shed? It is the one occasion when the fire was an expression of sorrow and judgment. The fire was in the sword of the angel that kept them from the tree of life so that they would not be forever locked into that fallen state. The fire defended God's plan to redeem mankind by keeping man in a state that could be changed.

Genesis 3:22-24 (KJV) *22 And the LORD God said, Behold, the man is become as one of us, to know good and evil: and now, lest he put forth his hand, and take also of the tree of life, and eat, and live forever: 23 Therefore the LORD God sent him forth from the garden of Eden, to till the ground from whence he was taken. 24 So he drove out the man; and he placed at the east of the garden of Eden Cherubims, and a flaming sword which turned every way, to keep the way of the tree of life.*

How sad that the first supernatural display of fire was to divide man from the place of fellowship, but actually his sin had already done that. From this time forward man would hunger for what Adam lost. Men would seek to fill the empty place within their hearts. Nothing in the flesh realm could possibly satisfy the soul of man. That God shaped hole was fitted perfectly to his Savior, Jesus. God had made a way but it took over 4000 years for it to be accomplished on the earth.

Genesis 4:10 *And he said, What hast thou done? the voice of thy brother's blood crieth unto me from the ground.*

Cain And Able Offerings

Adam's sons brought an offering to the Lord. Two brothers came before the Lord with different kinds of gifts. God is very concerned with only two things: passion and obedience; they are both rooted in the blood and produce the fire. First of all, He desires our hearts, our love, and our relationship with him and secondly, He requires that we do things as He instructed.

Genesis 4:3-7 (KJV) *3 And in process of time it came to pass, that Cain brought of the fruit of the ground an offering unto the LORD. 4 And Abel, he also brought of the firstlings of his flock and of the fat thereof. And the LORD had respect unto Abel and to his offering: 5 But unto Cain and to his offering he had not respect. And Cain was very wroth, and his countenance fell. 6 And the LORD said unto Cain, Why art thou wroth? and why is thy countenance fallen? 7 If thou doest well, shalt thou not be accepted? and if thou doest not well, sin lieth at the door. And unto thee shall be his desire, and thou shalt rule over him.*

When Abel brought his lamb to God, it was an act of obedience. He came to worship and sacrifice God's way. The animal was a symbol of the price of sin, and atonement was made by blood. The fire fell in response to the blood. Holy fire consumed the sacrifice and with it the sin was again covered, and punishment was suspended. There was a visible response that showed God accepted his sacrifice. The fire answered the blood offered on the altar. It is likely that Adam had taught both of his sons that sin required a blood sacrifice. We can assume that both men had it in their hearts to offer something of worth to God. The offering of grain was a portion of the harvest that Cain worked to produce, but it did not please God. No fire from heaven consumed Cain's sacrifice. While it did represent his efforts, it must have been a heart issue that caused Cain to approach God his own way. He may have been religious but he was not righteous. Religion is the attempt of man to reach God on his own terms. Redemption however, is the act of God reaching out to man and bringing him into relationship. Religion is never enough to make us acceptable to God. He made a way for us, and He expects us to come to him by following his designated route. We can never work hard enough or give enough to buy right standing with God. Peace with God is always by the shedding of blood.

Andrew Murray said in his book The Power of the Blood of Jesus that the fire falling was to bear witness that Abel pleased God. "His faith, and God's good pleasure in him, are closely connected with the sacrificial blood. In the light of later revelation, this testimony, given at the very beginning of human history, is of deep significance. It shows that there can be no approach to God, no fellowship with Him by faith, no enjoyment of His favor, apart from the blood." (Murray p. 9) When Cain brought an offering of grain, it was from the ground that was cursed because of sin. He was refusing to come by way of the blood. "The results of sin cannot be covered by a harvest of the best that human hands can produce. Along with the rest of the race, Cain stood under the sentence of death; and the only way out of that was for another to take his place, a life offered up and blood poured out on his behalf." (Smith p. 106) It is a waste of effort to try to come to God through human endeavor. The One, who is the Way, offered his own blood for us. Jesus loved mankind too much to leave us in our fallen state. He would rather die than live without us. Nothing but the blood was precious enough to offer as a ransom, or to buy salvation.

THERE IS FIRE IN THE BLOOD

Matthew 16:26 (KJV) *26 For what is a man profited, if he shall gain the whole world, and lose his own soul? or what shall a man give in exchange for his soul?*

Psalm 49:6-8 (KJV) *6 They that trust in their wealth, and boast themselves in the multitude of their riches; 7 None of them can by any means redeem his brother, nor give to God a ransom for him: 8 (For the redemption of their soul is precious, and it ceaseth for ever:)*

We see that the blood of the lamb was acceptable to God. When Cain saw God receive his brother's sacrifice he responded in anger and jealousy. Those works of the flesh led him to murder his own brother. Cain had refused to shed blood on the altar, but once the sin in his heart led to action, he shed blood in an unholy manner. The Bible tells us that God knew what happened and He said that instead of a lamb's blood crying mercy now Abel's blood was calling for justice. **Genesis 4:10 (KJV)** *10 And he said, What hast thou done? the voice of thy brother's blood crieth unto me from the ground.* His blood bore testimony to his brother's sin and demanded punishment.

We are told we can come to God freely because the blood of Jesus still speaks. The Blood of Jesus does not demand payment—it is payment in full to purchase all of mankind. There is no more sin debt. There is however, a sinner debt left within those who refuse his offer of forgiveness. **Hebrews 12:23-24 (KJV)** *23 To the general assembly and church of the firstborn, which are written in heaven, and to God the Judge of all, and to the spirits of just men made perfect, 24 And to Jesus the mediator of the new covenant, and to the blood of sprinkling, that speaketh better things than that of Abel.* The blood of Jesus cries reconciliation and mercy, it speaks the same words He spoke on the cross, *"It is finished,"* and the sin debt is canceled. All who will may claim that debt cancellation.

Colossians 2:13-15 (KJV) *13 And you, being dead in your sins and the uncircumcision of your flesh, hath he quickened together with him, having forgiven you all trespasses; 14 Blotting out the handwriting of ordinances that was against us, which was contrary to us, and took it out of the way, nailing it to his cross; 15 And having spoiled principalities and powers, he made a shew of them openly, triumphing over them in it.*

Are we offering something related to the blood of Jesus when we come before God? Our feeble attempts to obtain righteousness though religion or good works will never be enough to satisfy our souls. Mankind must find a way back into real relationship with God.

Religion in and of itself is destructive. Even though they were in the priesthood, Aaron's sons made the mistake of approaching God on their own terms, and by their own efforts. Many animals had been offered on the altar, blood was shed and then the fire fell from heaven and consumed the sacrifices. When they had just seen the manifestation of God, [Lev. 9], they took it upon themselves to bring what God called strange fire and it brought death. Aaron's sons did not honor God with their efforts because they did not follow God's instructions and approach in the prescribed manner.

Leviticus 10:1-2 (KJV) *1 And Nadab and Abihu, the sons of Aaron, took either of them his censer, and put fire therein, and put incense thereon, and offered strange fire before the LORD, which he commanded them not. 2 And there went out fire from the LORD, and devoured them, and they died before the LORD.*

We know that nothing in us is acceptable without the blood. No effort of man is enough. The Lord does not take it lightly when we try to earn our own way. Any time we ignore the blood and jump right to the manifestation, we have entered into religion. We would do well to offer whatever works we do as evidence of the fact that we are the blood bought and the blood washed children of God. It was not and never will be anything we do that makes us righteous, but only what He has done cleanses the soul of man.

Romans 3:22-26 (KJV) *22 Even the righteousness of God which is by faith of Jesus Christ unto all and upon all them that believe: for there is no difference: 23 For all have sinned, and come short of the glory of God; 24 Being justified freely by his grace through the redemption that is in Christ Jesus: 25 Whom God hath set forth to be a propitiation through faith in his blood, to declare his righteousness for the remission of sins that are past, through the forbearance of God; 26 To declare, I say, at this time his* *righteousness: that he might be just, and the justifier of him which believeth in Jesus.*

James 2:17 (KJV) *17 Even so faith, if it hath not works, is dead, being alone.* Faith in the blood of Jesus that produces nothing of substance in us is dead. In contrast, works alone without an understanding of the work of Christ and his blood shed for us will only produce frustration and exhaustion.

God never intended for man to remain stuck in his fallen state. Neither did He plan for mankind to struggle to obtain mercy. He expected men to come to him by faith and be changed. **Romans 8:29 (KJV)** *29 For whom he did foreknow, he also did predestinate to be conformed to the image of his Son, that he might be the firstborn among many brethren.*

His blood in our lives should produce his fruit in the earth. **Galatians 5:22-25 (KJV)** *22 But the fruit of the Spirit is love, joy, peace, longsuffering, gentleness, goodness, faith, 23 Meekness, temperance: against such there is no law. 24 And they that are Christ's have crucified the flesh with the affections and lusts. 25 If we live in the Spirit, let us also walk in the Spirit.* True faith in God is anchored to the blood. Out of gratitude, the heart of man produces works to honor the One who shed it.

2 Corinthians 3:17-18 (KJV) *17 Now the Lord is that Spirit: and where the Spirit of the Lord is, there is liberty. 18 But we all, with open face beholding as in a glass the glory of the Lord, are changed into the same image from glory to glory, even as by the Spirit of the Lord.* We are never to be like Cain who envied his brother and the result was death. On the contrary, we are to cling to God and become more and more like him. We are to change, being conformed to his image lest the blood shed for us be in vain. We are called to walk in love, in obedience and in reverence of the One who took our place.

Deuteronomy 7:9 *Know therefore that the LORD thy God, he is God, the faithful God, which keepeth covenant and mercy with them that love him and keep his commandments to a thousand generations;*

Walking in the Blood

Abraham is credited as the father of the faithful, a man who believed God and received great blessings because of it. We see him begin his faith walk in Genesis 12. God gave him one command and a series of blessings that would accompany his obedience.

Genesis 12:1-3 (KJV) *1 Now the LORD had said unto Abram, Get thee out of thy country, and from thy kindred, and from thy father's house, unto a land that I will shew thee:* [one command] *2 And I will make of thee a great nation, and I will bless thee, and make thy name great; and thou shalt be a blessing: 3 And I will bless them that bless thee, and curse him that curseth thee: and in thee shall all families of the earth be blessed.* There were seven promises that came with his obedience. God obligated himself to a man, and Abram [Abraham] believed God and went. He did not just obey God, but he held to the expectation that his obedience would bring the blessing. Abraham lived by the promises of God, not just the command. He expected to be blessed because the God who cannot lie had spoken it. Abraham's confidence led him to act as if the promise was already fulfilled.

Abraham was 75 years old when he first received the promise of a son. His wife was elderly too, and she was barren—she could not have a child when she was 20 let alone so late in life. God had promised. No matter how long it took, God would keep his word. Abraham was 100 when Isaac was born. He held to the promise of God for 25 years until the promise became manifestation. I am sure there were days when his faith was weak, but he never gave up. Even when it seemed hopeless Abraham still believed. When the manifestation was delayed, Abraham went to God with his concerns.

Genesis 15:2-8 (KJV) *2 And Abram said, Lord GOD, what wilt thou give me, seeing I go childless, and the steward of my house is this Eliezer of Damascus? 3 And Abram said, Behold, to me thou hast given no seed: and, lo, one born in my house is mine heir.* His relationship with God made him comfortable enough to say in general terms, "You promised I would be the father of a nation and here I am with no sons and according to custom, my servant will inherit everything I have." *4 And, behold, the word of the LORD came unto him, saying, This shall not be thine heir; but he that shall come forth out of thine own bowels shall be thine heir. 5 And he brought him forth abroad, and said, Look now toward heaven, and tell the stars, if thou be able to number them: and he said unto him, So shall thy seed be.* God made the promise so vivid that it inspired Abram to take hold of the promise anew. *6 And he believed in the LORD; and he counted it to him for righteousness. 7 And he said unto him, I am the LORD that brought thee out of Ur of the Chaldees, to give thee this land to inherit it. 8 And he said, Lord GOD, whereby shall I know that I shall inherit it?* God did not have to give him any further proof or promise but He did something very unusual; God entered into a blood covenant with this man.

Covenant is more than a contract; it is a powerful agreement that binds both parties together as one. Marriage, when lived out as God intended, is a form of covenant. Covenant comes from the Hebrew word *berith*. "In the Scriptures, it is the ultimate expression of committed love and trust and was usually made to define, confirm, establish, or make binding a relationship that had been in the making for some time." (Smith p. 12) We know Abraham had an ongoing relationship with God, but the covenant would solidify and formalize that walk with God. "A covenant is a binding, unbreakable obligation between two parties, based on unconditional love sealed by blood and sacred oath, which creates a relationship in which each party is bound by specific undertakings on each other's behalf. The parties to the covenant place themselves under the penalty of divine retribution should they later attempt to avoid those undertakings. It is a relationship that can only be broken by death."

(Smith p. 12, 13) Now that I know what a covenant entails, I am even more astonished that the Almighty God would enter into such an agreement with a fallen, mortal man. By sealing this agreement in blood, God was essentially promising that He would keep the promise forever. It would stand as long as the Eternal God lived. God bound his own existence with the covenant blood. It was that strong.

Genesis 15:9-10 (KJV) *9 And he said unto him, Take me an heifer of three years old, and a she goat of three years old, and a ram of three years old, and a turtledove, and a young pigeon.* Each animal named here would later become an acceptable sacrifice under the Mosaic Law. God was giving Abram a glimpse of his plan for the people of God. This was a portion of the law which He intended to reveal through Moses. The essence of the Mosaic Law was bound to the sacrifices. Every blood sacrifice represented the Lamb of God that takes away the sin of the world. *10 And he took unto him all these, and divided them in the midst, and laid each piece one against another: but the birds divided he not.* This was a customary way of cutting covenant. Men from the nations around him performed this same kind of ceremony. By walking through the blood they were saying if I break my word and stop defending and standing with you, an enemy has the right to come in and split my body in half and march between the pieces at the defeat I brought upon myself. It was a serious matter to cut the covenant. It was a holy commitment even when executed between men. Abram knew it was no small thing that the Almighty God would covenant with a mere man.

Genesis 15:11-18 (KJV) *11 And when the fowls came down upon the carcases, Abram drove them away.* What he had offered to God could not be defiled by birds of prey. The blood flowed freely. Abram had obeyed. The fire did not fall the moment the blood was shed, but he waited, and he protected the sanctity of that offering. *12 And when the sun was going down, a deep sleep fell upon Abram; and, lo, an horror of great darkness fell upon him...* God revealed to Abraham that he would have a son, that he would become a great nation and that his people would end up as slaves in Egypt. God even revealed some of his plan to free them and his timeline. *17 And it came to pass, that, when the sun went down, and it was dark, <u>behold a smoking furnace, and a burning lamp that passed</u>*

between those pieces. **There was fire in the blood.** *18 In the same day the LORD made a covenant with Abram...*God showed up in person, a flame of fire and walked in the blood with Abram.

In the process of cutting the animals apart and offering them to God, the blood got on Abraham. Then, when God passed between the pieces, both of them had walked in the blood. Blood must always be on the one identified with the death of the sacrifice. The blood on Abraham meant he was under the provision of the entire covenant, and all it covered was already his in the spirit. Abraham walked through the covenant blood and in addition to the inheritance of land, it was enough to both produce and preserve his son's life. It established a linage that would lead all the way to Jesus.

Walking through the blood symbolized a new era. It showed that Abraham considered this a new life. It was as if he was dead to his previous life and he would walk from that day forward with God. It was a faith journey that he entered into. In his heart it was almost as powerful as a resurrection; it was a type of being born again.

Deuteronomy 7:9 (KJV) *9 Know therefore that the LORD thy God, he is God, the faithful God, which keepeth covenant and mercy with them that love him and keep his commandments to a thousand generations;* "God's act of initiating covenant and then His fulfilling of every promise made in the covenant is an act of grace and mercy renewed every day." (Smith p. 50) That covenant reaches through time to us.

Hebrews 6:13-14 (KJV) *13 For when God made promise to Abraham, because he could swear by no greater, he sware by himself, 14 Saying, Surely blessing I will bless thee, and multiplying I will multiply thee.*

Cutting the covenant covered more than Abraham knew. It was powerful in his lifetime, but it meant even more in the heart of God. Creating a body uncontaminated by Adam's blood was no small feat. I know that when God got Abraham to enter into covenant that He was working toward that goal. Covenanting with Abraham was an entrance strategy into the earth. When Abraham offered his only son, the son of the promise, on an altar it made way for God, his covenant partner, to do the same thing. I am certain that it was essential that there be a reciprocal action that allowed God's Son entrance to the earth. The world needed a Savior and God would do whatever was required to bring mankind back from their fallen state. This was an important step toward fulfilling the promise to bring salvation to the world. God had already determined that the death of Jesus would cleanse every heart that his blood touched.

I thought about that blood on Abraham and then I remembered something that was said when Jesus was condemned to die. **Matthew 27:22-25 (KJV)** *22 Pilate saith unto them, What shall I do then with Jesus which is called Christ? They all say unto him, Let him be crucified. 23 And the governor said, Why, what evil hath he done? But they cried out the more, saying, Let him be crucified. 24 When Pilate saw that he could prevail nothing, but that rather a tumult was made, he took water, and washed his hands before the multitude, saying, I am innocent of the blood of this just person: see ye to it. 25 Then answered all the people, and said, <u>His blood be on us, and on our children.</u>*

It is interesting to me that while they meant "We accept the responsibility for his death," God was doing something entirely different with the words they spoke. What could have been a curse became a door to blessing. If only they would apply the blood of Jesus to their own lives, they too could enter into covenant like Abraham did. By faith they could take the blood that poured from his wounds and start afresh. They could truly be born again, their sins completely forgiven by his substitute sacrifice. The Holy Blood of God's Lamb could seal their inheritance. If they believed the promises and provisions made in that blood, it would change them forever. The blood applied by faith would produce a fire to continually burn within them.

The Bible is a blood covenant. Every promise in scripture was made to us. All of its benefits are secured by the Father God, confirmed in the blood of Jesus, and received in the heart of man. I pray that his blood is upon you. He alone can testify that you have that blood in your life and use it to manifest his glory in your behalf.

Hebrews 9:22 (NLT) *For without the shedding of blood, there is no forgiveness.*

God Provides His Own Lamb

We have already stated that Abraham and God had a blood covenant. The act of entering into that covenant bound them to respond in kind to what their partners asked or did. I call it a reciprocal obligation. Neither God nor Abraham could ask of the other what they were not willing to give. After all those years of waiting, Abraham now possesses the son of the promise. Every time he looks at his son, he has to think that is the miracle—that is the faithfulness of God at work for me. His heart and even his faith are bound in the life of Isaac. God is about to put his covenant partner to the test. Does Abraham love the gift of his son more than the giver?

Genesis 22:1-18 (KJV) *1 And it came to pass after these things, that God did tempt Abraham, and said unto him, Abraham: and he said, Behold, here I am. 2 And he said, Take now thy son, thine only son Isaac, whom thou lovest, and get thee into the land of Moriah; and offer him there for a burnt offering upon one of the mountains which I will tell thee of.* Isaac was the one God had promised and his life held all the generations of the future that God had pledged to Abraham. Isaac's death would mean an end to that heritage and the promise of God. Could Abraham trust God with so much at stake? God, his covenant partner, said offer your only begotten son on the altar. If Abraham obeyed, then God could do the same. *3 And Abraham rose up early in the morning, and saddled his ass, and took two of his young men with him, and Isaac his son, and clave the wood for the burnt offering, and rose up, and went unto the place of which God had told him.* We see no sign of rebellion in Abraham; he quickly obeyed. He walked with God, and taught his son to do the same. This was undoubtedly not the first time Isaac accompanied him as he went to offer sacrifice. *4 Then on the third day Abraham lifted up his eyes, and saw the place afar off.* I believe he saw in the spirit, into the future sacrifice of God's own son. There is a chance that the place he saw and the place he offered Isaac was Calvary. *5 And Abraham said unto his young men, Abide ye here with the ass; and I and the lad will go yonder and worship, and come again to you.* Knowing he was about to slit the throat of his own son, he tells his servants, "We will be back." He knew Isaac was the son of the promise. If Isaac died without children the promise of God would die too. He knew the One he walked in covenant with could not and would not lie. Somehow Isaac would live again. That was truly a gift of faith to be confident enough to act on God's command with so much at stake. *6 And Abraham took the wood of the burnt offering, and laid it upon Isaac his son; and he took the fire in his hand, and a knife; and they went both of them together.* Isaac carried the wood for the sacrifice, just like Jesus carried his own wooden cross. They both carried the wood toward their destiny. *7 And Isaac spake unto Abraham his father, and said, My father: and he said, Here am I, my son. And he said, Behold the fire and the wood: but where is the lamb for a burnt offering? 8 And Abraham said, <u>My son, God will provide himself a lamb</u> for a burnt offering: so they went both of them together.* God had always planned for Jesus to be the Lamb of God—the ultimate sacrifice. Abraham said prophetically what John would announce hundreds of years later, "Behold the Lamb of God." *9 And they came to the place which God had told him of; and Abraham built an altar there, and laid the wood in order, and bound Isaac his son, and laid him on the altar upon the wood.* Isaac was not a small boy. He was most likely a young man. Abraham was well over 100 years old. If Isaac did not willingly allow the sacrifice, I am sure he could have escaped. Like Jesus, he trusted in God and willingly lay down his life on the altar. It was an act of obedience to both God and Abraham, his father. *10 And Abraham stretched forth his hand, and took the knife to slay his son.* Abraham fully intended to kill his son, and that was enough to allow it bring the reciprocal action of his covenant partner. *11 And the angel of the LORD called unto him out of heaven, and said, Abraham, Abraham: and he said, Here am I. 12 And he said, Lay not thine hand upon the lad, neither do thou any thing unto him: for now I know that thou fearest God, seeing thou hast not withheld thy son, thine only son from me.* God always cares about the heart in action, and He saw in Abraham a heart of full obedience. *13 And Abraham lifted up his eyes, and looked, and behold behind him a ram caught in a thicket by his horns: and Abraham went and took the ram, and offered him up for a burnt offering in the stead of his son.* It was not a lamb, it was a ram. The Lamb God would provide was Jesus, His only begotten son. *14 And Abraham called the name of that place Jehovahjireh: as it is said to this day, In the mount of the LORD it shall be seen. 15 And the angel of the LORD called unto Abraham out of heaven the second time, 16 And said, By myself have I sworn, saith the LORD, for because thou hast done this thing, and hast not withheld thy son, thine only son: 17 That in blessing I will bless thee, and in multiplying I will multiply thy seed as the stars of the heaven, and as the sand which is upon the sea shore; and thy seed shall possess the gate of his enemies; 18 And in thy seed shall all the nations of the earth be blessed; because thou hast obeyed my voice.* The entire world would have access to God because in the days to come, Jesus the Lamb of God would be slain. All men would have a sacrifice to bring them into the covenant. Every act of obedience on Abraham's part made way for us to be saved.

We know that according to the New Testament, Abraham believed if necessary there would be a resurrection. **Hebrews 11:17-19 (KJV)** *17 By faith Abraham, when he was tried, offered up Isaac: and he that had received the promises offered up his only begotten son, 18 Of whom it was said, That in Isaac shall thy seed be called: 19 Accounting that God was able to raise him up, even from the dead; from whence also he received him in a figure.* That confidence in God made the resurrection of Jesus a direct response to faith in the covenant as well.

We have a God who cannot fail and who is faithful towards us. **2 Corinthians 1:20 (KJV)** *20 For all the promises of God in him are yea, and in him Amen, unto the glory of God by us.* We can trust in the strength of the covenant that God has with man in the person of Jesus. Just like Abraham, we can take every promise of God and see it stronger than the demands of this life. Any request from God is part of His plan and we should trust and obey. Abraham could not have known this promise, but we do. **Romans 8:28 (KJV)** *28 And we know that all things work together for good to them that love God, to them who are the called according to his purpose.* God was working out something infinitely more important for the whole of the world when He called his covenant partner to lay down the life of his precious son. He was preparing to offer up the perfect sacrifice.

From Passover To Passing Over

Moses taught captive Israel how to use sacrificial blood to break out of bondage and set themselves apart as God's own people. As the spokesman for God he led them into a closer relationship with the God of their fathers and established the covenant that became known as Passover. First the blood was shed and then the corresponding fire came the next day when they were driven out of Egypt. God in the form of a pillar of fire stood between his covenant partners and their enemies.

Exodus 12:21-23 (KJV) *21 Then Moses called for all the elders of Israel, and said unto them, Draw out and take you a lamb according to your families, and kill the passover.* The penalty for sin was death. Justice demanded that the guilty die. God in his mercy allowed a substitute. "Life was possible for them only through the blood of a life given in their place, and appropriated by the sprinkling of that blood." (Murray p.11) *22 And ye shall take a bunch of hyssop, and dip it in the blood that is in the bason, and strike the lintel and the two side posts with the blood that is in the bason; and none of you shall go out at the door of his house until the morning. 23 For the LORD will pass through to smite the Egyptians; and when he seeth the blood upon the lintel, and on the two side posts, the LORD will pass over the door, and will not suffer the destroyer to come in unto your houses to smite you.* Death was and still is the result of God's judgment on sin. The

Passover was the tenth and final plague that brought judgment against Egypt. In his book, <u>Power in the Blood</u>, Charles Spurgeon called Passover an act of salvation by blood. (p. 43) God said to take the substitute blood of an innocent lamb and to recognize that the only reason judgment and death did not touch them was that God had accepted this blood in place of their sons.

At Passover, the blood was placed on the entrance of their homes. He told them to take a branch of Hyssop, a particularly limp and absorbent plant, and to use it like a paintbrush. Hyssop was the means of applying the blood so it has become symbolic of faith. The blood has always been applied by faith. It was painted first on the beam above the door and then on each door post. The action of painting it formed the sign of the cross on which Jesus would die. They were subject to judgment because they were the sons of Adam, but God had chosen his own Son to be the Lamb slain from the foundation of the world. All of the members of the family would openly show that they believed the blood would save them, by walking through that blood cross. They entered in by way of the blood and it kept them safe while destruction touched everyone outside of the blood covenant. "The avenger was to demand a life, but the life was already paid, for there was the blood to prove it." (Spurgeon p. 44) In answer to their faith in the blood, an angel hovered over their homes and kept away the spirit of death that took every first born male from the smallest sheep to the son of pharaoh. That blood stood between them and the power that would destroy and became a shield to them.

Passover was God saying the devil can never touch the ones covered in covenant blood. The Jews used a token lamb for each house and as the destroyer came, that bloodline would not allow even their animals to be killed. God saw the blood applied by faith and reached into the spirit to the blood of Jesus the true lamb slain from the foundation of the earth. God the righteous judge found them not guilty of death by virtue of the blood of Jesus. The token blood of a lamb was visible proof of their covenant relationship with God as their protector and deliverer. No mere animal sacrifice could do what they needed, but the true blood and faith in their God was more than sufficient.

THERE IS FIRE IN THE BLOOD

No matter what the need, the blood is enough to identify you with his death and resurrection; his righteousness is imparted to you. When you get saved the blood is upon you. God never sees the stain of sin on you when He looks through the blood! You look clean. You look like the One who died for you.

The children of Israel did as commanded. They kept the Passover and at midnight when the whole of Egypt went into mourning, they were at peace. The word came from pharaoh that they were to leave at once. They picked up their belongings and headed toward the Promised Land, but they went by way of the place where God had spoken to Moses from the burning bush. They had obeyed God by shedding blood and then the fire appeared.

Exodus 13:21-22 (KJV) *21 And the LORD went before them by day in a pillar of a cloud, to lead them the way; and by night in a pillar of fire, to give them light; to go by day and night: 22 He took not away the pillar of the cloud by day, nor the pillar of fire by night, from before the people.* There it is. That is the fire that came after they had applied the blood. God shows up and leads them personally through the wilderness. He stands there as a shield against the heat of day. The fire of his presence burns all night. They have evidence that He is with them, guiding them and they just follow the fire. Every single man woman and child could see the manifest presence of God with them. What a comfort it must have been for the ones fleeing slavery to see they were not alone.

Just when they were starting to enjoy their freedom and getting comfortable following the fire, things changed. Pharaoh's mourning had turned to anger. He wanted vengeance and his labor force back. The most powerful army in the world was marching toward them. The moment they were in danger, the fire got between them and the attacking army. That is what the Lord does for his covenant partners. He will be a guide to lead, but when needed He will also become a powerful force to defend.

Exodus 14:19-20 (KJV) *19 And the angel of God, which went before the camp of Israel, removed and went behind them; and the pillar of the cloud went from before their face, and stood behind them: 20 And it* *came between the camp of the Egyptians and the camp of Israel; and it was a cloud and darkness to them, but it gave light by night to these: so that the one came not near the other all the night.* God stood between them and sure death. They had nowhere to run, and nowhere to hide except beneath the shadow of the Almighty. At that point, God opened a path for them through the Red Sea. He gave them a way of escape and fought for them, destroying all of the army that opposed them. They had believed in the protective power of the blood at Passover and now they were seeing God's corresponding action as the One in the Fire came to their defense.

The same Holy Spirit, who is your comforter, will also defend you should you need him. When I had my first real job, I worked in a bridal shop as a saleswoman and seamstress. One day, a very tall man came into the shop and asked to see some wedding dresses for his fiancé, who lived in another state; after selecting one, he made an unusual request that I model the gown. The owner said it was a reasonable request and to comply, which I did. On his next visit, he asked to try on a gown himself, which was both strange and totally unacceptable. He said he had lied before and was in a play and needed a dress, and matching shoes. He made everyone very uncomfortable. After his third trip in we decided he should shop elsewhere and I asked him to leave. The following morning I came in early and opened the shop. I always arrived first and was used to being alone until we opened. When I had unlocked the doors, I began working in the cutting room. I heard the bell on the front door. We were not technically open, but I went out expecting a customer. There stood that same man. He walked up to me, got in my face and with an angry, raspy voice said, "We are going in the fitting room." I responded "I don't think so." He pulled out a rope, wound it around both fists, placed it at my throat and said in a louder more persistent voice, "We are going in the back room." None of the images in my mind about his intentions seemed good. In that moment I heard these words come out of my spirit, the place where that comforter, the Holy Spirit dwells, "In the name of Jesus Christ whose I am and whom I serve, I command every foul spirit to leave." The Holy Spirit who rose up within me backed that attacker out the door and he ran away. My boss came in shortly after that and when I told her what had happened, she called the police. They never did find him, but a report was filed, and I looked at a lot of mug shots. The girls

THERE IS FIRE IN THE BLOOD

who worked with me started answering the door with a pair of scissors in their hand when they were alone, but I was never afraid because the one who had washed me in the blood had become a fire shut up in my bones that rose up and defended me when needed. **The blood is still powerful enough to produce the fire!**

Hebrews 9:22 (KJV) *22 And almost all things are by the law purged with blood; and without shedding of blood is no remission.*

Consecration And Dedications

Adam's sin tainted everything on earth. When something was determined to be holy, it had to be purified, sanctified, and consecrated for the Lord's use. When the blood was applied the item was cleansed. These are just a few examples of how the blood set apart priests and the tabernacle and the temple for holy use. Everything was sprinkled with blood. Frequently, the blood was accompanied by an anointing oil, and of course the power of the Holy Spirit answered with fire. When we see the power of God present in such an amazing way, it makes us hungry for more. We want to be near him, to feel his fire in our hearts and in our worship services. We have the shed blood of Jesus and our hearts cry out for the fire of the Holy Spirit.

Those in closest proximity to the Lord were consecrated first. The priests were dressed in special clothing, anointed with oil and then they shed blood. They were finally identified with the blood of the sacrifices. They started by consecrating the altar. **Leviticus 8:14-16 (KJV)** *14 And he brought the bullock for the sin offering: and Aaron and his sons laid their hands upon the head of the bullock for the sin offering. 15 And he slew it; and <u>Moses took the blood,</u> and put it upon the horns of the altar round about* with his finger, and <u>purified the altar, and poured the blood at the bottom of the altar, and sanctified it, to make reconciliation upon it.</u> *16 And he took all the fat that was upon the inwards, and the caul above the liver, and the two kidneys, and their fat, and Moses burned it upon the altar.* It does not say Moses set a fire; God sent the fire, just like in the days of Abel.

Next, the priests were anointed and commissioned. **Leviticus 8:22-24 (KJV)** *22 And he brought the other ram, the ram of consecration: and Aaron and his sons laid their hands upon the head of the ram. 23 And he slew it; and <u>Moses took of the blood of it, and put it upon the tip of Aaron's right ear, and upon the thumb of his right hand, and upon the great toe of his right foot.</u> 24 And he brought Aaron's sons, and Moses put of the blood upon the tip of their right ear, and upon the thumbs of their right hands, and upon the great toes of their right feet: and Moses sprinkled the blood upon the altar round about.* First he anointed the ear with blood, so they would hear the voice of the Lord. Then he moved on to their thumbs, representing the work they would do. Finally, he put blood on the toe, because they had to walk daily in the office of the priesthood. Their covenant relationship with God was intended to influence every aspect of their lives and service.

In the same way, Christians are touched by the blood. Once the blood of Jesus is on you, it affects how you hear his written and spoken word, and you begin to know his voice. His blood affects what your hands find to do and your walk with the Lord. Having been cleansed, you are ready for the anointing. **It is always the blood first and then the spirit.**

The pattern God set up worked in my life; He applied the blood to my ear, to my hands and to my walk. First, I heard the Gospel presented and I got saved. I had no religious training or background. He anointed my ear to hear, and I began to understand his Word. He placed a hunger in my heart for more of Him. He anointed my hands, and I began to work for the Lord and the church. At first I ran the nursery, and I taught children. Later, I led the Baptist Young Women's group for my church, and eventually for the whole county. I learned sign language at church, and eventually interpreting became both a calling and a career that touched countless deaf individuals. Some of them are in the kingdom of God now, because I was called to minister as an interpreter. I was filled with the precious Holy Spirit and soon after that, God called me to minister his Word. I became a licensed and ordained evangelist. I later decided to get my degree in Christian Ministry. I love preaching in the church and at revivals and conferences. I also teach adult Sunday school. I can honestly say that my walk is drastically different now than it was when He first touched me. Everything in my life was touched by the blood and the fire.

We know the life in his blood makes men, who were common and unclean, holy. It was the blood of animals that was used to consecrate everything of spiritual use in the tabernacle and the temple. Those things do not have the value of people. God wanted more than a home on the earth. He wanted a home in the hearts of his people; the covenant was always about God getting men back into his presence. The whole idea was to make mankind righteous again. He started with the priesthood, but He wanted the whole of humanity back. God determined to break the sin barrier that separated him from the ones He loved. He never wanted a thick veil to hang between man and the glory. It was a protective shield for man until the blood was shed. **Matthew 27:50-51 (KJV)** *50 Jesus, when he had cried again with a loud voice, yielded up the ghost. 51 And, behold, the veil of the temple was rent in twain from the top to the bottom...* The moment Jesus died, God said in effect, "I am opening the door and man is coming home; man is coming back into my presence." Fellowship is possible because Jesus shed his blood for us.

You are consecrated by the blood of Jesus. You are set apart for holy use. You are anointed for service. It is you that He chose as a royal priesthood. **Exodus 19: 5 (KJV)** *5 Now therefore, if ye will obey my voice indeed, and keep my covenant, then ye shall be a peculiar treasure unto me above all people: for all the earth is mine:* He spoke that not only over Israel in the Old Testament, but also over Christians in the New Testament. **1 Peter 2:9 (KJV)** *9 But ye are a chosen generation, a royal priesthood, an holy nation, a peculiar people; that ye should shew forth the praises of him who hath called you out of darkness into his marvellous light:*

God consecrated Aaron and his sons as priests for eight days before they presented any offerings. God took their sanctification for office seriously. The blood made them clean. What happened immediately in the spirit took time for man to grasp. The priests and the whole of the congregation of Israel needed to recognize the blood as a changing force. They needed to honor the office of the priesthood. God prepared them for service, and then told them to get the rest of his people under the covering of blood.

God told them to bring all the sacrifices and pour out the blood and then the fire and the glory of the LORD would show up. They brought a calf, a kid, goats, a bullock and a ram. **Leviticus 9:4-7 (KJV)** *4 ... for today the LORD will appear unto you. 5 And they brought that which Moses commanded before the tabernacle of the congregation: and all the congregation drew near and stood before the LORD. 6 And Moses said, This is the thing which the LORD commanded that ye should do: <u>and the glory of the LORD shall appear unto you</u>. 7 And Moses said unto Aaron, Go unto the altar, and offer thy sin offering, and thy burnt offering, and make an atonement for thyself, and for the people: and offer the offering of the people, and make an atonement for them; as the LORD commanded.*

There were more sacrifices made that day, both atonement and peace offerings. The Lord responded to all that blood by manifesting his glory. **Leviticus 9:23-24 (KJV)** *23 And Moses and Aaron went into the tabernacle of the congregation, and came out, and blessed the people: and the glory of the LORD appeared unto all the people. 24 <u>And there came a fire out from before the LORD, and consumed upon the altar the burnt offering and the fat: which when all the people saw, they shouted, and fell on their faces</u>.* First the blood then the fire, the same pattern was evident throughout the Bible. If you wanted the presence of God, you offered a blood sacrifice. Remember, the life is in the blood so when a life was given in the natural, supernatural life showed up. We still want that. Jesus shed his precious blood for us and now we who are sanctified by that blood make a place for Him in our hearts. We honor the blood and worship the One who shed it and we wait for Him to come and fill us.

Each time Moses set up the tabernacle in the wilderness the pattern held. Consecrate everything with blood and then the fire and the glory of God will do the rest. **Exodus 40:29 (KJV)** *29 And he put*

THERE IS FIRE IN THE BLOOD

the altar of burnt offering by the door of the tabernacle of the tent of the congregation, and <u>offered upon it the burnt offering</u> and the meat offering; as the LORD commanded Moses.

Exodus 40:34-38 (KJV) *34 Then a cloud covered the tent of the congregation, and <u>the glory of the LORD filled the tabernacle</u>. 35 And Moses was not able to enter into the tent of the congregation, because the cloud abode thereon, and the glory of the LORD filled the tabernacle. 36 And when the cloud was taken up from over the tabernacle, the children of Israel went onward in all their journeys: 37 But if the cloud were not taken up, then they journeyed not till the day that it was taken up. 38 <u>For the cloud of the LORD was upon the tabernacle by day, and fire was on it by night, in the sight of all the house of Israel,</u> throughout all their journeys.*

It is recorded in the New Testament as well. **Hebrews 9:19 - 22 (KJV)** *19For when Moses had spoken every precept to all the people according to the law, he took the blood of calves and of goats, with water, and scarlet wool, and hyssop* [Remember hyssop represents faith.]*, and <u>sprinkled both the book, and all the people,</u> 20 Saying, This is the blood of the testament* [or covenant] *which God hath enjoined unto you. 21Moreover he sprinkled with blood both the tabernacle, and all the vessels of the ministry. 22And <u>almost all things are by the law purged with blood; and without shedding of blood is no remission.</u>*

The nation of Israel grew strong, but their awareness of God waivered. Over time, they stopped seeking God passionately. They were led by prophets and judges and eventually they chose to put their trust in a king. **1 Samuel 8:7 (KJV)** *7 And the LORD said unto Samuel, Hearken unto the voice of the people in all that they say unto thee: for they have not rejected thee, but they have rejected me, that I should not reign over them.*

They took their focus off the spiritual and trusted in men. Their first king, Saul lost the kingdom through his rebellion against God. Then God called a man of faith to take the office. **Acts 13:22 (KJV)** *22 And when he had removed him, he raised up unto them David to be their king; to whom also he gave testimony, and said, I have found David the son of Jesse, a man after mine own heart, which shall fulfil all my will.*

King David loved the Lord, and wanted to bring the Ark of the Covenant back to Jerusalem. That Ark represented the presence of God and that presence was precious. I have heard that the priests claimed that a blue white flame appeared between the cherubim, above the Mercy Seat. David did not seek some idol or symbol. He wanted to be near the God of Israel. David determined in his heart to honor God, and to worship as he went. He danced before the Lord. When the Levites had carried the Ark six paces, they stopped so he could offer sacrifices. They walked for about 12 miles, stopping every six paces to set up a makeshift altar. The priests killed countless animals for burnt offerings. He would dance and offer up worship, and the blood of hundreds of animals poured out like a river all along the road he traveled. [2 Samuel 6:12-18] David understood that the blood and the fire were connected; he wanted the presence of God. He set up a tabernacle for the Ark, and went there to meet with God. It was just a tent but the fire of God burned there upon the Mercy Seat. David had such a heart for God that he wanted to build a more permanent temple, a place to honor God and offer sacrifices. He gathered wood and stone and storehouses full of gold and silver for the work, but the work was passed on to his son, Solomon.

Solomon recognized he could not really make a place on earth for the God who created it. He had the right attitude, a humble heart, and a determination to make the temple of God glorious. **2 Chronicles 2:6 (KJV)** *6 But who is able to build him an house, seeing the heaven and heaven of heavens cannot contain him? who am I then, that I should build him an house, save only to burn sacrifice before him?* He knew that God was to be honored and he felt small in comparison to the task. Solomon remembered the relationship his father David had with God and he humbled himself to seek to honor God. Solomon's temple was a masterpiece but it was just an empty shell until the blood flowed from the altar and the Lord moved in.

2 Chronicles 5:11-14 (KJV) *11 And it came to pass, when the priests were come out of the holy place... 13 It came even to pass, as the trumpeters and singers were as one, to make one sound to be heard in praising and thanking the LORD; and when they lifted up their voice with the trumpets and cymbals and instruments of musick, and praised the LORD, saying, For he is good; for his mercy endureth for ever: that then <u>the house</u>*

THERE IS FIRE IN THE BLOOD

was filled with a cloud, even the house of the LORD; 14 So that the priests could not stand to minister by reason of the cloud: for the glory of the LORD had filled the house of God.

2 Chronicles 7:1-3 (KJV) *1 Now when Solomon had made an end of praying, the fire came down from heaven, and consumed the burnt offering and the sacrifices; and the glory of the LORD filled the house. 2 And the priests could not enter into the house of the LORD, because the glory of the LORD had filled the LORD'S house. 3 And when all the children of Israel saw how the fire came down, and the glory of the LORD upon the house, they bowed themselves with their faces to the ground upon the pavement, and worshipped, and praised the LORD, saying, For he is good; for his mercy endureth for ever.*

Like Solomon's temple, we are just an empty shell until He moves in and fills us with the Glory. We come to God by means of the blood. We do not just want to look good on the outside. We want to be full of him. The blood of the Way, the Truth and the Life still produces an inferno. **John 14:6 (KJV)** *6 Jesus saith unto him, I am the way, the truth, and the life: no man cometh unto the Father, but by me.* As a believer, I still hunger for God to fill my house, my life with more and more of his spirit.

1 Corinthians 6:19-20 (KJV) *19 What? know ye not that your body is the temple of the Holy Ghost which is in you, which ye have of God, and ye are not your own? 20 For ye are bought with a price: therefore glorify God in your body, and in your spirit, which are God's.* By virtue of the blood, He moved into a new Holy of Holies. You are now the temple of God and He wants to live within you. Look to the blood and find the flame within.

1 Kings 18:39 (KJV) *39 And when all the people saw it, they fell on their faces: and they said, The LORD, he is the God; the LORD, he is the God.*

God's Fire When The Wood Is Wet

God has never been satisfied with casual relationships or half-hearted connections to him. The Hebrew people had grown cold and indifferent and had incorporated the worship of other so called "gods" into their daily lives. In short, they had made light of their covenant relationship. They acted as if God was no longer powerful, almost as if He was no different from the idols around them. God would not allow them to stay in that compromised state. His prophet, Elijah, called the people together and asked them to make a commitment to follow God completely or sever their ties to the Lord and worship idols. **Victory on Mt. Carmel would decide who was really LORD in Israel.** Elijah took on the 450 prophets of Baal in a contest for the loyalty of the people. It was a winner take all gamble and there was no doubt in the mind of Elijah; God would prevail.

1 Kings 18:21 (KJV) *21 And Elijah came unto all the people, and said, How long halt ye between two opinions? if the LORD be God, follow* *him: but if Baal, then follow him. And the people answered him not a word.* Their silence did not quench his faith. He stated the obvious, there were many religious zealots for Baal, and there was one man who knew he had a covenant with the Almighty. Any time it is just one man and God, that man is in the majority. Standing with God makes him powerful.

1 Kings 18:22-28 (KJV) *22 Then said Elijah unto the people, I, even I only, remain a prophet of the LORD; but Baal's prophets are four hundred and fifty men. 23 Let them therefore give us two bullocks; and let them choose one bullock for themselves, and cut it in pieces, and lay it on wood, and put no fire under: and I will dress the other bullock, and lay it on wood, and put no fire under: 24 And call ye on the name of your gods, and I will call on the name of the LORD: and <u>the God that answereth by fire, let him be God</u>. And all the people answered and said, It is well spoken.* The people agreed to his terms. *25 And Elijah said unto the prophets of Baal, Choose you one bullock for yourselves, and dress it first; for ye are many; and call on the name of your gods, but put no fire under. 26 And they took the bullock which was given them, and they dressed it, and called on the name of Baal from morning even until noon, saying, O Baal, hear us. But there was no voice, nor any that answered. And they leaped upon the altar which was made. 27 And it came to pass at noon, that Elijah mocked them, and said, Cry aloud: for he is a god; either he is talking, or he is pursuing, or he is in a journey, or peradventure he sleepeth, and must be awaked. 28 And they cried aloud, and cut themselves after their manner with knives and lancets, till the blood gushed out upon them.* Those 450 men cried out, and made foolish gestures and even spilled their own blood next to their sacrifice, but there was no answer. All their worldly attempts to bring about a manifestation fell flat. Absolutely nothing happened. They should have known flesh can never bring about anything of spiritual value. No mere idol has the power to bring supernatural fire. Their failure was obvious to all, but that alone would not sway the people.

It was not enough for Baal to be weak; the LORD must be proven strong. **1 Kings 18:30-35 (KJV)** *30 And Elijah said unto all the people, Come near unto me. And all the people came near unto him. And he repaired the altar of the LORD that was broken down.* Elijah was "old-school" he went back to their roots. He took a stone for each tribe that came from

THERE IS FIRE IN THE BLOOD

the loins of Abraham's grandson Jacob and he built an altar where faith and sacrificial blood and the power of God could all be displayed. He was reminding them of former covenants. Elijah knew he was calling upon the same God who had entered into covenant with Abraham and Isaac and Jacob. *31 And Elijah took twelve stones, according to the number of the tribes of the sons of Jacob, unto whom the word of the LORD came, saying, Israel shall be thy name: 32 And with the stones he built an altar in the name of the LORD: and he made a trench about the altar, as great as would contain two measures of seed. 33 And he put the wood in order, and cut the bullock in pieces, and laid him on the wood,* He shed blood. He did it at the time of the evening sacrifice. If he had stopped there and prayed and fire fell it would have been powerful, but he wanted to be sure that everyone knew there was a God in Israel who could do the miraculous. *and said, Fill four barrels with water, and pour it on the burnt sacrifice, and on the wood.* By the time Elijah was finished, there was no way any man could have started a fire in the natural. He made it impossible so they would recognize the One who does the impossible. Only the power of God could get that wood to burn. I have a fireplace in my living room and I can tell you that even damp wood will not burn. *34 And he said, Do it the second time. And they did it the second time. And he said, Do it the third time. And they did it the third time. 35 And the water ran round about the altar; and he filled the trench also with water.* The prophet was not afraid to put God to the test. That was twelve barrels full of water, which seems like overkill to me. From what we see in the next few verses, Elijah was following instructions. Faith and presumption are two entirely different things. He did not act on his own, but he responded with obedience to the only One who could prove his lordship. Everything was soaked and there was a moat surrounding the altar. Elijah knew the God he served was more than able to answer with fire.

1 Kings 18:36 - 39 (KJV) *36And it came to pass at the time of the offering of the evening sacrifice, that Elijah the prophet came near, and said, LORD God of Abraham, Isaac, and of Israel, let it be known this day that thou art God in Israel, and that I am thy servant, and that I have done all these things at thy word.* He asked for the glory. It was not a long prayer; there was no worship music or any other religious activity. He simply called upon the Lord and the Lord answered him. *37Hear me, O LORD, hear me, that this people may know that thou art the LORD*

God, and that thou hast turned their heart back again. <u>*38 Then the fire of the LORD fell,*</u> *and consumed the burnt sacrifice...* That is enough for me. The fire answered the blood and the cry of a man who believed in the power of the blood. Read that again. *38 Then the fire of the LORD fell, and consumed the burnt sacrifice, and the wood, and the stones, and the dust, and licked up the water that was in the trench.* That supernatural fire that fell was so hot and so powerful it destroyed every remnant of what had been the altar. Stone and dirt and all the water in that trench were consumed by the flame. There was nothing left but a scorched plot of ground. *39 And when all the people saw it, they fell on their faces: and they said, The LORD, he is the God; the LORD, he is the God.*

Elijah offered the sacrifice and then <u>holy fire consumed the sacrifice and the doubts of the people</u>. God's power is greater than any of us can understand. God showed himself great in the eyes of an unworthy and unbelieving people to turn their hearts back to him. If the devil had known that his 450 minions were outnumbered by one man of faith, he would not have let them meet there on Mount Carmel.

How much more has God outdone himself to show us that He loves us? He proved He was willing to do anything to bring us back into fellowship with him. He sent his own Son in our stead. Jesus walked among common men. He looked like everyone else. He was all man on his mother's side, but pure divinity on the Father's side. The perfect intermediary was sent to establish the covenant.

The Jewish priesthood did not recognize the Lord when He walked among men. While they prayed for the Messiah to come, the very One they prayed for was walking in their streets, healing their sick, and teaching in their synagogues. They had a covenant with God and yet they went to the temple and slit the throats of countless lambs while the Lamb of God was dying on a cross. They rejected the One sent to redeem them. If they so easily overlooked him then, why would the world recognize him now?

As a whole, society still rejects the One sent to them. Men rely on their own warped sense of morality. In our society, we see the spirits of compromise and complacency too often. People are trying to follow what is politically correct and socially acceptable as if sin no longer matters and the Word of God is no longer pertinent. I was around when they took prayer out of school, and declared that God was dead. In recent years, they have tried to remove "In God We Trust" from our currency and "One nation under God" from the Pledge of Allegiance. They have legalized homosexual marriage, and abortion, as if the majority saying that it is right makes it so. The enemy has been bold but the LORD is still God and his truth will always prevail. There will never be a time when we do not need the Savior.

2 Corinthians 4:1-4 (KJV) *1 Therefore seeing we have this ministry, as we have received mercy, we faint not... 3* <u>*But if our gospel be hid, it is hid to them that are lost: 4 In whom the god of this world hath blinded the minds of them which believe not, lest the light of the glorious gospel of Christ, who is the image of God, should shine unto them.*</u> The world around us does not see and know the truth; they do not recognize their need for God. They have tried to wipe out the name of God and ignored his precious blood.

2 Timothy 3:1-5 (KJV) *1 This know also, that in the last days perilous times shall come. 2 For men shall be lovers of their own selves, covetous, boasters, proud, blasphemers, disobedient to parents, unthankful, unholy, 3 Without natural affection, trucebreakers, false accusers, incontinent, fierce, despisers of those that are good, 4 Traitors, heady, highminded, lovers of pleasures more than lovers of God; 5 Having a form of godliness, but denying the power thereof: from such turn away.* That is a pretty accurate account.

The world may be a dark place with many hearts growing cold, but there is still hope for the lost. There are still a few Elijahs out there. God still has faithful men and women who cling to the truth. I have had the privilege to sit at the feet of a few of those preachers and teachers. I have known men of great faith and integrity. I am writing this because an anointed man of faith with a prophetic word confirmed that I am called to share in print what God has revealed to me. God's truth, His words will outlast all of us.

The blood of Jesus was above and beyond what man deserved. It was a plan so great that the Bible called it a mystery. The power to become the sons of God was more than any mortal man could have hoped for and more than the enemy thought possible.

1 Corinthians 2:6-10 (KJV) *6 Howbeit we speak wisdom among them that are perfect: yet not the wisdom of this world, nor of the princes of this world, that come to nought: 7 But we speak the wisdom of God in a mystery, even the hidden wisdom, which God ordained before the world unto our glory: 8 Which none of the princes of this world knew: for <u>had they known it, they would not have crucified the Lord of glory</u>. 9 But as it is written, Eye hath not seen, nor ear heard, neither have entered into the heart of man, the things which God hath prepared for them that love him. 10 But God hath revealed them unto us by his Spirit: for the Spirit searcheth all things, yea, the deep things of God.* The devil did not know that killing Jesus would bring so many men and women to God or he would not have faced off with God on Calvary. He threw his best punch—death, but it could not hold Jesus. On the third day, when Jesus rose again, death was forever defeated. Mankind was free because the sin debt was paid in full.

1 Corinthians 2:12 (KJV) *12 Now we have received, not the spirit of the world, but the spirit which is of God; that we might know the things that are freely given to us of God.* It was a mystery that the world largely overlooked, but He revealed it to us. God called us into the truth, and into his family. He built a church based on the crucified and resurrected Lord.

God still wants the whole heart of man. He was not content with the state of the Israelites in Elijah's day, and He is not going to tolerate a lukewarm church. [See Rev. 3:14-20] In our day, man has become indifferent and self-sufficient again. The average man may attend church, but God is not the center of his life. People do not realize how much they need God.

A friend of mine told me she dreamed that there were thousands of people lined up at the gates of heaven. The good and the bad offered their reasons why they should be allowed to enter. One said she had attended church her whole life and taught Sunday school for 35 years. Another said he had fed the poor, and another said he had fought social injustice as a public defender. Others had been nurses and doctors. There were teachers and police officers, and store keepers. One by one, they laid out their good deeds, but none of them could enter heaven. One man said he was a religious man, and that all religions lead to heaven. He too, left disappointed. A woman stood in protest saying only an unjust God would send anyone to hell. Another raged against society, and racial inequality, stating he had already lived through hell on earth. One by one their claims were refused, all except one man. He said, "I did nothing worthy of entrance, but I come on the basis of another; I plead the blood of Jesus who died for me." That brought the perfect response, *"Enter thou in, thou good and faithful servant."* We can never earn a right standing with God. Our only hope is in the One who poured out his lifeblood for us.

Jesus made it clear that no man can be saved by his own righteousness, but that all can call upon the Lord and receive mercy. **Luke 18:9-14 (KJV)** *9 And he spake this parable unto certain which trusted in themselves that they were righteous, and despised others: 10 Two men went up into the temple to pray; the one a Pharisee, and the other a publican. 11 The Pharisee stood and prayed thus with himself, God, I thank thee, that I am not as other men are, extortioners, unjust, adulterers, or even as this publican. 12 I fast twice in the week, I give tithes of all that I possess. 13 And the publican, standing afar off, would not lift up so much as his eyes unto heaven, but smote upon his breast, saying, God be merciful to me a sinner. 14 I tell you, this man went down to his house justified rather than the other: for every one that exalteth himself shall be abased; and he that humbleth himself shall be exalted.*

The wicked and the righteous alike were lavished with an offering that was more than enough. Any man can cry out for forgiveness. Any man can say, "The Lord, He is God. I was lost and without hope in the world. God personally purchased my freedom through the death, burial and resurrection of Christ. I plead the blood of Jesus." All who call upon the name of the Lord will be saved. It is never about us, it is all about Jesus; it is all about the blood.

Romans 5:8 *But God commendeth his love toward us, in that, while we were yet sinners, Christ died for us.*

Holy Blood On The Altar Of The Cross

What is it about blood? People are fascinated by blood. There seems to be a theme of it that runs from Genesis to Revelation. I have heard it referred to as the scarlet thread of redemption. In Genesis there is the shedding of animal blood to cover Adam and Eve, followed by the first sacrifice and the first murder. In Leviticus, the law is given with very precise rules about how to offer sacrificial blood. Then there were thousands of sacrifices all based on the corrective value of blood. There is the genealogy of Christ, because his blood line mattered. Finally there is the holy blood of Christ poured out on Calvary. It is that sacrificial, holy bloodline that we follow right into heaven.

Leviticus 17:10-11 (KJV) *11 For the life of the flesh is in the blood: and I have given it to you upon the altar to make an atonement for your souls: for it is the blood that maketh an atonement for the soul.*

"Life itself is spiritual, but it must have a physical carrier, and this carrier is the blood." (Whyte p. 14) If just any human blood of a righteous man would do, Abel would have put an end to sin and the death that came with it. Regular blood, like that in Abel was never sufficient. It could never satisfy the demands of justice. The blood in his veins was tainted, contaminated by sin. Even though he had not personally rebelled against God in the Garden, his father had. The penalty for sin and the corruption that accompanied it was passed down through every child of Adam. Blood is the carrier for human life, but it can also carry spiritual life or death. When Adam sinned, mankind was forever changed; sin was passed on to every generation. **1 Corinthians 15:22 (KJV)** *22 For as in Adam all die, even so in Christ shall all be made alive.* Life and death were in the blood. No man born from Adam's race could possibly be our redeemer. Since Jesus was not conceived by any human father, we know that the blood in him was uncontaminated by the sin of Adam. The life of God was in the blood of Jesus and once shed it could be transfused into any willing vessel.

Jesus, like Adam was not born from the seed of man, but came into this world by direct action from God. Neither of them had natural blood from an earthly father. Their blood was created without human assistance. It was essential that there be a virgin birth. Jesus could not become the final sacrifice if there was any trace of Adam's blood and the sin it carried, in him. Listen to what was written immediately after the fall of Adam. **Genesis 3:14-15 (KJV)** *14 And the LORD God said unto the serpent, Because thou hast done this, thou art cursed above all cattle, and above every beast of the field; upon thy belly shalt thou go, and dust shalt thou eat all the days of thy life: 15 And I will put enmity between thee and the woman, and between thy seed and her seed; it shall bruise thy head, and thou shalt bruise his heel.* There is no seed in the natural within the woman, but the Lord had a plan to bring Jesus that was first spoken in the Garden of Eden. It included one without the seed of Adam. If we truly believe the Bible, we have to conclude that the blood in Jesus was the blood of God.

The Lord sent an angel to the Virgin Mary with the promise of that One who would become our redeemer. **Luke 1:30-38 (KJV)** *30 And the angel said unto her, Fear not, Mary: for thou hast found favour with God. 31 And, behold, thou shalt conceive in thy womb, and bring forth a son, and shalt call his name JESUS. 32 He shall be great, and shall be called the Son of the Highest: and the Lord God shall give unto him the* *throne of his father David: 33 And he shall reign over the house of Jacob for ever; and of his kingdom there shall be no end. 34 Then said Mary unto the angel, How shall this be, seeing I know not a man? 35 And the angel answered and said unto her, The Holy Ghost shall come upon thee, and the power of the Highest shall overshadow thee: therefore also that holy thing which shall be born of thee shall be called the Son of God... 38 And Mary said, Behold the handmaid of the Lord; be it unto me according to thy word. And the angel departed from her.* She believed the Word of God spoken to her. Those words had enough creative power in them to bring life. Her faith allowed the preexistent Son of God to take on a flesh and blood body. It was that body that would be the atoning sacrifice for the whole of mankind.

John 1:14 (KJV) *14 And the Word was made flesh, and dwelt among us, (and we beheld his glory, the glory as of the only begotten of the Father,) full of grace and truth.*

Hebrews 2:14-17 (KJV) *...14 Forasmuch then as the children are partakers of flesh and blood, he also himself likewise took part of the same; that through death he might destroy him that had the power of death, that is, the devil; 15 And deliver them who through fear of death were all their lifetime subject to bondage. 16 For verily he took not on him the nature of angels; but he took on him the seed of Abraham. 17 Wherefore in all things it behoved him to be made like unto his brethren, that he might be a merciful and faithful high priest in things pertaining to God, to make reconciliation for the sins of the people.*

Hebrews 10:5 (KJV) *5 Wherefore when he cometh into the world, he saith, Sacrifice and offering thou wouldest not, but a body hast thou prepared me:* [See Isaiah 9:5-7 and Matthew 1:18-25] "The life that flowed in the veins of the Lord Jesus Christ came from God. No wonder He said I am the Life. God imparted his own life into the Bloodstream of Jesus." (Whyte p.17) Only holy blood could be poured out as a willing substitute for mankind. Every heathen religion demanded blood, but our God provided blood. What an awesome gift! Jesus willingly gave his own blood for us.

Psalm 40:6-8 (KJV) *6 Sacrifice and offering thou didst not desire... 7 Then said I, Lo, I come: in the volume of the book it is written of me, 8 I delight to do thy will, O my God...* Jesus came to become the sacrifice that every lamb foreshadowed. He came as the one and only possible solution for the sins of man. The whole of scriptures declared He was coming and then pointed him out.

The disciples and the people they originally wrote to had a working knowledge of crucifixion. They were eye witnesses, but what they recorded was not as detailed as we would have liked. The following few verses contain the general information of how His precious blood was spilled.

John 19:17-18 (KJV) *And they took Jesus, and led him away. 17 And he bearing his cross went forth into a place called the place of a skull, which is called in the Hebrew Golgotha: 18 Where they crucified him, and two other with him, on either side one, and Jesus in the midst.* He stretched out his arms and they hammered nails into his hands and feet. He hung on the cross for hours, taunted and reviled, struggling for every breath.

John 19:30 (KJV) *30...Jesus therefore had received the vinegar, he said, It is finished: and he bowed his head, and gave up the ghost...*

Mark 15:37-39 (KJV) *37 And Jesus cried with a loud voice, and gave up the ghost. 38 And the veil of the temple was rent in twain from the top to the bottom. 39 And when the centurion, which stood over against him, saw that he so cried out, and gave up the ghost, he said, Truly this man was the Son of God.*

John 19:33-34 (KJV) *33 But when they came to Jesus, and saw that he was dead already, they brake not his legs: 34 But one of the soldiers with a spear pierced his side, and forthwith came there out blood and water he said, Truly this man was the Son of God.* The saving blood of God's sacrifice fell from the hands and feet that were pierced for us; the droplets rained down upon the soldiers below. Holy blood gushed from his side. The blood was shed, the price was paid; once and for all justice was satisfied. The redemption of man was complete. Jesus spoke the same words that the High Priest spoke when the last acceptable lamb was brought to be slain in the temple courtyard. *"It is finished."*

The life is in the blood—the very life of Jesus is in the shed blood. We know all that He did and the power that He had is still in that blood. First and foremost, salvation is in that blood. Right standing with God is possible because it was shed. Healing is in that blood, resurrection power is in it, and deliverance from demons. It is all still in the blood. It is because of that very blood that we can ask for help in the time of need because the blood has never lost its power. He who loved us so very much that He died for us is still present when we call upon the blood.

John the Baptist spoke prophetically of Jesus being the Lamb of God and his substitutionary sacrifice. "Notice, first, that when John the Baptist announced His coming, he spoke of Him as filling a dual office: as *"the Lamb of God that taketh away the sin of the world,"* and then as *"the One who would baptize with the Holy Spirit."* The outpouring of the blood of the Lamb of God must take place, before the outpouring of the Spirit could be bestowed. Only when all that the Old Testament taught about the blood has been fulfilled, can the dispensation of the Spirit begin." (Murray p 14-15) There it is again, the divine order was always the blood and then the fire of the Holy Spirit.

We know it was planned for the Son to, "...join humanity in their sinful condition, taking their place and bearing their sin in His body, pouring out His life blood for them as them. Before time and space were created, the ultimate gift of the sacrifice of the Son had already been given in the heart and determination of God." (Smith p. 102) It was that perfect sacrifice that was represented by every animal that died on the altar. Let me say that another way. <u>The blood of Jesus slain from the foundation of the earth, was presented again each time an animal died on the altar.</u> The blood of those animals was useless unless it pointed to the cross. **Hebrews 10:4 (KJV)** *4 For it is not possible that the blood of bulls and of goats should take away sins.* Every animal sacrifice was a type drawing man to the real Lamb of God, Jesus, who would be the perfect and final sacrifice to be offered on the altar of the cross.

In his book, <u>The Power of the Blood of Jesus</u>, Andrew Murray speaks of the difference between the animals sacrificed and Jesus. He notes that the value of the blood corresponds to the value of the life that is in it. The life of a man is more valuable than that of many sheep. The life of Abel meant more to God than the life of the lamb he offered, but the life of Jesus was even more precious. Jesus was the first God-man. He was fully human, but He was sin-free. He had always existed and when He walked the earth He was God incarnate. He was there when Adam was created and when Adam fell. This One that was fully God limited himself and came to earth in the form of frail humanity. Within Jesus dwelt the soul of the holy Son of God. "The eternal life of the Godhead was carried in that Blood." (Murray p.27) His blood was more valuable than the blood of every righteous man who ever lived. "His blood was in itself of infinite value, because it carried His soul or life. But the atoning virtue of His blood was infinite also, because of the manner in which it was shed. In holy obedience to the Father's will, He subjected Himself to the penalty of the broken law by pouring out His soul unto death. By that death not only was the penalty borne, but the law was satisfied, and the Father glorified. His blood atoned for sin, and thus made it powerless." (Murray p. 28-29) **1 Corinthians 15:55 (KJV)** *55 O death, where is thy sting? O grave, where is thy victory?* His blood was enough to cancel the power and the fear of death.

When we look at Hebrews we see the value God put on the cross and the blood of Christ. Countless animal sacrifices could only postpone the penalty of sin. They never destroyed the power of sin or satisfied the demands of justice. Only the blood of Jesus would keep mankind from the judgment he faced.

Hebrews 9:12 (KJV) *12 Neither by the blood of goats and calves, but by his own blood he entered in once into the holy place, having obtained eternal redemption for us.*

Hebrews 9:14 (KJV) *14 How much more shall the blood of Christ, who through the eternal Spirit offered himself without spot to God, purge your conscience from dead works to serve the living God?*

THERE IS FIRE IN THE BLOOD

Hebrews 10:19-22 (KJV) *19 Having therefore, brethren, boldness to enter into the holiest by the blood of Jesus, 20 By a new and living way, which he hath consecrated for us, through the veil, that is to say, his flesh; 21 And having an high priest over the house of God; 22 Let us draw near with a true heart in full assurance of faith, having our hearts sprinkled from an evil conscience, and our bodies washed with pure water.*

Hebrews 12:24 (KJV) *24 And to Jesus the mediator of the new covenant, and to the blood of sprinkling, that speaketh better things than that of Abel.* Having just read these scriptures, it is clear that the blood was powerful and priceless. "The Holy Spirit teaches us that the blood is really the central power of our entire redemption." (Murray p. 17) Isaiah and Hebrews are two of my favorite books in the Bible, because they are virtually saturated in the blood. There is no more powerful topic. It is by virtue of the blood that we can stand before God forgiven and clean.

In Adam, all of mankind for all generations was condemned to die, but in Jesus we enter into a new Creation. "He enters into and walks our history into the death where sin had put us, and in resurrection joins us to His history carrying us into union with the Father." (Smith p. 77) **1 Corinthians 15:20-22 (KJV)** *20 But now is Christ risen from the dead, and become the firstfruits of them that slept. 21 For since by man came death, by man came also the resurrection of the dead. 22 For as in Adam all die, even so in Christ shall all be made alive.*

When we choose to be born again, we enter into covenant with God. We come alone, with nothing to offer as an excuse for our sin. We come with no offering except the one God provided. That blood opens the door into fellowship with God, joining us together in perfect unity. **1 Corinthians 6:17 (KJV)** *17 But he that is joined unto the Lord is one spirit.* "Jesus is God coming to where we are, joining us in our lost condition without being lost Himself, taking to Himself our death and carrying us out in His resurrection. We now must be united to Him, partake of His life and strength, and be taken into intimate fellowship with Him where He is." (Smith p. 138) The hope of the world was sent to die for us. There was enough power in the blood of Jesus to wash clean every fallen soul. **1 Timothy 2:4-6 (KJV)** *4 Who will have all men to be saved, and to come* *unto the knowledge of the truth.* <u>*5 For there is one God, and one mediator between God and men,*</u> *the man Christ Jesus; 6 Who gave himself a ransom for all, to be testified in due time.* Jesus is forever the bridge between God and man. Since He was the perfect representative of both the Godhead and humanity, He could reach from the one to the other, with the intent of reuniting them.

Identification Is Our Response

God always intended for man to be redeemed. His plan for our salvation began before the world we live in was made. God had already covenanted with Jesus to take on flesh and blood and with it the role of the sacrificial lamb before He placed Adam in the Garden. God was not shocked or surprised when Adam fell; He was fully prepared. Jesus was both willing and eager to shed his blood in order to restore fellowship with the whole of mankind. Once provision was made, it was the responsibility of man to accept that blood as payment for his own sin. That is called identification.

Jesus intentionally took our place. His death meant man could live. A great exchange was available to all who would receive it. **2 Corinthians 5:21 (KJV)** *21 For he hath made him to be sin for us, who knew no sin; that we might be made the righteousness of God in him.* Jesus did not just pay my bill; He took my sin within him, actually becoming the embodiment of sin. In him, all sin was judged and sentence was passed upon it. When the fullness of that sin brought death, all was paid. Justice was met. The prophet Isaiah looked down through time and caught a glimpse of the cross and recorded it for us.

Isaiah 53:4-12 (KJV) *4 Surely he hath borne our griefs, and carried our sorrows: yet we did esteem him stricken, smitten of God, and afflicted. 5 But he was wounded for our transgressions, he was bruised for our iniquities: the chastisement of our peace was upon him; and with his stripes we are healed. 6 All we like sheep have gone astray; we have turned every one to his own way; and the LORD hath laid on him the iniquity of us all. 7 He was oppressed, and he was afflicted, yet he opened not his mouth: he is brought as a lamb to the slaughter, and as a sheep before her shearers is dumb, so he openeth not his mouth. 8 He was taken from prison and from judgment: and who shall declare his generation? for he was cut off out of the land of the living: for the transgression of my people was he stricken. 9 And he made his grave with the wicked, and with the rich in his death; because he had done no violence, neither was any deceit in his mouth. 10 Yet it pleased the LORD to bruise him; he hath put him to grief: when thou shalt make his soul an offering for sin, he shall see his seed, he shall prolong his days, and the pleasure of the LORD shall prosper in his hand. 11 He shall see of the travail of his soul, and shall be satisfied: by his knowledge shall my righteous servant justify many; for he shall bear their iniquities. 12 Therefore will I divide him a portion with the great, and he shall divide the spoil with the strong; because he hath poured out his soul unto death: and he was numbered with the transgressors; and he bare the sin of many, and made intercession for the transgressors.* What a beautiful, insightful picture of the cross. The Amplified Bible says, *10 "When you and He make Him an offering for sin [and He has risen from the dead, in time to come]..."* When you identify with the sacrifice it becomes powerful enough to cleanse you and satisfy God. The prophet said He was killed that many could live and that his death pleased God. It only pleased God because man now had potential salvation and restoration.

On earth, that process started on the Mount of Olives. It was there Jesus prayed so earnestly for us that He sweat blood. **Matthew 26:36 (KJV)** *36 Then cometh Jesus with them unto a place called Gethsemane, and saith unto the disciples, Sit ye here, while I go and pray yonder.* **Matthew 26:38-39 (KJV)** *38 Then saith he unto them, My soul is exceeding sorrowful, even unto death: tarry ye here, and watch with me. 39 And he went a little further, and fell on his face, and prayed, saying, O my Father, if it be possible, let this cup pass from me: nevertheless not as I* *will, but as thou wilt.* When Jesus spoke of drinking from the cup, it was the cup of the covenant. If there was any other means of redemption it would have been offered, but there was not. Jesus would take on all the sins of mankind, embracing the filth of the world that separated God and man. Jesus did not sweat blood over the pain He would face. Man's fallen nature and the enormity of sin that He must embody caused him to struggle. The Holy One of Israel became sin for us. All that was evil would fit inside the Son of God and be carried before the spirit world where sin would be judged. Jesus knew the Father would have to turn away while He hung on the cross. He knew He would become separated from God the Father for the first time since eternity began. It was not a surprise that He would be forsaken while his lifeblood drained from his flesh. Spiritual death would claim a third of the Trinity. This was the cup of the covenant that Jesus must drink if man went free. **Matthew 26:42 (KJV)** *42 He went away again the second time, and prayed, saying, O my Father, if this cup may not pass away from me, except I drink it, thy will be done.*

The blood was never meant to be a generic offering for the faceless masses. If we are to partake of the power that is in the blood, it has to be personalized, I must identify with the blood shed for me. I was the one who sinned. I was the guilty one standing beneath the cross needing the very life-giving drops that fell from his body. I was lost and alone and stood naked before God. I needed salvation and redemption and I had to apply the blood to my own life. I had to see myself as I was, dirty and broken. If I could understand my need and cry out for mercy, I could change my eternal destiny.

On November 1, 1972, I realized I needed to be saved. I went to a revival at Suburban Baptist Church. The service was concluding and the minister said, "If you died right now and know that you would be in heaven, raise your hand." I could not do it. I tried to raise my hand but it would not obey. I wanted to think that I would be okay but I was not ready to face God. I had heard the scriptures that day and for the first time, I knew I was lost. So I found myself kneeling at the front of the church crying out for forgiveness. I confessed every sin I could remember and I knew I was dependent upon the One who died for me. My life was flawed, damaged by sin. I needed him. I said, "My life is a mess but if you can do anything with it, you can have it." I was not versed in church jargon. I did not know to call it being "saved" or "born again," but I was free. I felt clean and whole for the first time in my life. I had identified with a dying Christ and been forgiven.

Every believer comes through faith in what Jesus did. We all identify with the shed blood by faith. God made sure the plan was clearly stated so we would not miss it. He lay out a map for us to follow in the scriptures.

Romans 3:23-26 (KJV) *23 For all have sinned, and come short of the glory of God; 24 Being justified freely by his grace through the redemption that is in Christ Jesus: 25 Whom God hath set forth to be a propitiation through faith in his blood, to declare his righteousness for the remission of sins that are past, through the forbearance of God; 26 To declare, I say, at this time his righteousness: that he might be just, and the justifier of him which believeth in Jesus.*

Romans 5:6-8 (KJV) *6 For when we were yet without strength, in due time Christ died for the ungodly. 7 For scarcely for a righteous man will one die: yet peradventure for a good man some would even dare to die. 8 But God commendeth his love toward us, in that, while we were yet sinners, Christ died for us.*

Romans 10:8-13 (KJV) *8 But what saith it? The word is nigh thee, even in thy mouth, and in thy heart: that is, the word of faith, which we preach; 9 That if thou shalt confess with thy mouth the Lord Jesus, and shalt believe in thine heart that God hath raised him from the dead, thou shalt be saved. 10 For with the heart man believeth unto righteousness; and with the mouth confession is made unto salvation. 11 For the scripture saith, Whosoever believeth on him shall not be ashamed. 12 For there is no difference between the Jew and the Greek: for the same Lord over all is rich unto all that call upon him. 13 For whosoever shall call upon the name of the Lord shall be saved.* If we believe that, we are born again. Unfortunately, if we do not believe, we have no life in us and no hope.

THERE IS FIRE IN THE BLOOD

It is not enough that just anyone died for us. All men die. Jesus, the righteous Son of God, satisfied all the demands of justice. He was born without sin, and lived without sin. When He poured out his lifeblood for us, it paid for all of us. Jesus died as a substitutionary sacrifice. He went willingly into hell and stayed there until all was accomplished. Jesus entered into the realm of the eternal, where time had no boundaries, and He suffered there until every trace of sin was destroyed. He conquered sin and death in the depths of hell eliminating their power over mankind. Satan was defeated once and for all. Jesus did that for us. His blood permanently covered our sins. He paid the full price of sin so I would not have to do it, and then He also rose from the dead. "Once dead, only God can bring a person back to life. In the realm of the physical, He does that in the resurrection; and spiritually, He accomplishes it in the miracle of the new birth." (Smith p. 31) We can trust in what his death and resurrection have purchased for us and it will bring life to us. The resurrection is proof that death and hell can never hold us. His resurrection is the defining factor that separates Christianity from all other religions. The blood is legal basis for our claim on eternal life. It is the only hope for mankind in this troubled world.

Do you believe that He died for you and that He rose from the dead? Then do something about it. Until you identify with what He did, it will not benefit you. Your part is to simply believe and then act upon your beliefs.

The truth is there in the scriptures, written out for all to see and believe. I remember a story that illustrated the love and the sacrifice of Jesus in totally different terms. A young boy and his dad were riding in an old truck. It was a warm day and the windows were open. They were going fishing and the boy was happy and excited and talking a mile a minute. Suddenly, there was silence. The man looked over and saw a look of complete terror on his son's face. He was confused until he noticed a bee on the dashboard. His son was highly allergic to bee stings. If he were to be stung, he would most likely die. The dad reached over and grasped the bee. He held it in his hand for a moment and then threw it out the window. Then he said, "It's alright now son, I took the sting." That is what Jesus did—he took the sting of sin and death and all the pain and agony they brought. He bore the guilt, punishment and pain so we could be free. He died in our place and that is the only thing that made us holy and worthy to come before God and receive anything. He took the final judgment and the sting of death and overcame it.

Galatians 3:13 (KJV) *13 Christ hath redeemed us from the curse of the law, being made a curse for us...* The same God who created man, and wrote the law also satisfied the law. "The law demands death: **Ezekiel 18:4 (KJV)** *4 the soul that sinneth, it shall die.* Christ gave what the law demands, and more. Christ, my Lord, has died, died in my place." (Spurgeon p. 46) If Jesus died for me, then justice is satisfied; I am no longer worthy of the death penalty.

1 Peter 2:24 (KJV) *24 Who his own self bare our sins in his own body on the tree, that we, being dead to sins, should live unto righteousness: by whose stripes ye were healed."*

1 Timothy 2:4-6 (KJV) *4 Who will have all men to be saved, and to come unto the knowledge of the truth. 5 For there is one God, and one mediator between God and men, the man Christ Jesus; 6 Who gave himself a ransom for all, to be testified in due time.* "When God sees Blood, He does not see sin." (Whyte p.24) What are you doing with the blood that was shed for you? You can receive salvation and the forgiveness of sin that it bought, but God will never force you to do it. Salvation is a choice.

To be saved all you have to do is ask. Tell him that you are sorry for your sins and that you want to be forgiven. Repentance is a turning to God through the blood of Jesus and recognizing we need his gift of forgiveness. We do turn away from sin, but more than that we turn toward God. Tell him you believe in Jesus, that He died for you and that He rose from the dead. Believe in your heart that his blood paid for your sins and you will never have to live under the weight of those sins again.

Deuteronomy 30: 19 (KJV) *19 I call heaven and earth to record this day against you, that I have set before you life and death, blessing and cursing: therefore choose life, that both thou and thy seed may live*: Choose life; you can live free.

THERE IS FIRE IN THE BLOOD

Romans 10: 13 (KJV) *13 For whosoever shall call upon the name of the Lord shall be saved.*

1 John 2:1-2 (KJV) *1 My little children, these things write I unto you, that ye sin not. And if any man sin, we have an advocate with the Father, Jesus Christ the righteous: 2 And he is the propitiation for our sins: and not for ours only, but also for the sins of the whole world.* We all sin. Even if we lived a really good life, we would still need to be saved because we are part of Adam's race. Most of us can recall times when we failed, or openly rebelled. Everyone needs forgiveness.

We know that our attorney, our advocate, is the very same one who paid for our sin and so we can walk into the court of heaven and know that we will be spared. Double Jeopardy means you cannot be tried a second time for the same crime. If a crime has been committed and justice was paid, no further punishment is legal. Since I am in Christ, and since He paid for all sin, I know that what guilt was upon me and the punishment due me was placed on him. I just claim the blood already shed for my crimes and the judge has no choice but to honor the blood and let me go free. "God will never punish you for the same offense for which Jesus died. His justice will not permit Him to see the debt paid first by the surety, and then again by the debtor. Justice cannot demand recompense twice; if my bleeding Substitute has borne my guilt, then I cannot bear it. Accepting Christ Jesus as having suffered for me, I have accepted a complete discharge from judicial liability." (Spurgeon p. 23) It should be a great relief and a great comfort to know that God finds no fault in you.

If you are really born again, you have been made completely new. Your old man is dead and your history starts at the point of your salvation. **2 Corinthians 5:17-19 (KJV)** *17 Therefore if any man be in Christ, he is a new creature: old things are passed away; behold, all things are become new. 18 And all things are of God, who hath reconciled us to himself by Jesus Christ, and hath given to us the ministry of reconciliation; 19 To wit, that God was in Christ, reconciling the world unto himself, not imputing their trespasses unto them; and hath committed unto us the word of reconciliation.* That word reconciled, is the word **katallassō** Strong's Greek word #2644 and it means to be mutually changed, and to make a difference to both parties. That means it changed you and God's relationship to you. **Romans 8:1-2 (KJV)** *1 There is therefore now no condemnation to them which are in Christ Jesus, who walk not after the flesh, but after the Spirit. 2 For the law of the Spirit of life in Christ Jesus hath made me free from the law of sin and death.* We are free, loosed from the weight of guilt and shame. We should no longer fear our past or our future.

The Holy Spirit within us proves we are his. He also guarantees we have access to the whole of the provisions of salvation. **Ephesians 1:13-14 (KJV)** *13 In whom ye also trusted, after that ye heard the word of truth, the gospel of your salvation: in whom also after that ye believed, <u>ye were sealed with that holy Spirit of promise</u>, 14 Which is the earnest of our inheritance until the redemption of the purchased possession, unto the praise of his glory.*

Once saved you are made right with God. You are clean; you have applied the blood shed for you and are eligible for the fire. That is the infilling of his Holy Spirit.

II Corinthians 3:17-18 (KJV) *17 Now the Lord is that Spirit: and where the Spirit of the Lord is, there is liberty. <u>18 But we all, with open face beholding as in a glass the glory of the Lord, are changed into the same image from glory to glory, even as by the Spirit of the Lord.</u>* If we continually look to him we will become like him. It is the same glory that Adam lost. We have a way to get it back now that we are saved.

1 Corinthians 2:7-8 (KJV) *7 But we speak the wisdom of God in a mystery, even the hidden wisdom, which God ordained before the world unto our glory: 8 Which none of the princes of this world knew: for had they known it, they would not have crucified the Lord of glory.* "The Father of Glory [Eph. 1:17], sent the Lord of Glory to lift up the man who had been crowned with Glory, but had fallen from the Glory, back into the Glory of His Presence" (Brim p. 41) God wanted more than a once a week visitation with his children. He wanted us back in fellowship and his glory reinstated in us. "If Satan had seen the plan, he never would have lifted God's spotless Lamb to the altar of the Cross where His innocent

Blood could be shed to cleanse man to once again stand in the Glory of God's Presence." (Brim p. 41)

Colossians 1:26-27 (KJV) *26 Even the mystery which hath been hid from ages and from generations, but now is made manifest to his saints: 27 To whom God would make known what is the riches of the glory of this mystery among the Gentiles; which is <u>Christ in you, the hope of glory</u>:* How awesome is that? God wants us back in the Glory. "At our new birth, the process of glorification begins and progresses according to the plan as we look into God's Word for His glory and yield ourselves to the Holy Spirit." (Brim p. 42)

We were not just saved from judgment and death and hell, but we were saved to something. <u>We were saved to a restoration of the glory.</u> The blood of Jesus bought and paid for all that Adam lost and part of what he lost was the inner fire of the Holy Ghost that shone forth from him with the light of God's glory. While it cannot be seen in the flesh, we are being changed continually and the fullness of that glory will be revealed in us. "<u>For it is His Blood that cleanses us, and covers us, and enables us to stand in His glory.</u>" (Brim p. 43)

Acts 1:8 *But ye shall receive power, after that the Holy Ghost is come upon you:*

Pentecost

After the Lord rose from the dead, He gave the disciples instructions to wait and to receive an impartation of his spirit. They became believers when they trusted in the blood, but He wanted them to have the fire. He wanted them to experience God in a deeper way. Jesus wanted God inside the believers, empowering them. The cross was essential, but it was not the end. He died, but He also rose and because He did, He could begin to fill believers. Pentecost was always part of the plan.

He poured out his blood at Calvary so the Holy Spirit could be poured out at Pentecost. It is vital that we focus on the gift of the Holy Spirit in light of and response to what Jesus did on the cross. If we want a powerful outpouring of the Holy Ghost, we must look first to the cross and make much of the blood shed for us.

Acts 1:1-5 & 8 (KJV) *1 The former treatise have I made, O Theophilus, of all that Jesus began both to do and teach, 2 Until the day in which he was taken up, after that he through the Holy Ghost had given commandments unto the apostles whom he had chosen: 3 To whom also he shewed himself alive after his passion by many infallible proofs, being seen of them forty days, and speaking of the things pertaining to the kingdom of God: 4 And, being assembled together with them, commanded them* *that they should not depart from Jerusalem, but wait for the promise of the Father, which, saith he, ye have heard of me. 5 For John truly baptized with water; but ye shall be baptized with the Holy Ghost not many days hence... 8 But ye shall receive power, after that the Holy Ghost is come upon you: and ye shall be witnesses unto me both in Jerusalem, and in all Judaea, and in Samaria, and unto the uttermost part of the earth.* Jesus knew they would need fire within to share salvation effectively. They had the blood on them, but they needed the Holy Ghost within them.

Acts 2:1-4 (KJV) 1 And when the day of Pentecost was fully come, they were all with one accord in one place. 2 And suddenly there came a sound from heaven as of a rushing mighty wind, and it filled all the house where they were sitting. 3 And there appeared unto them cloven tongues like as of fire, and it sat upon each of them. 4 And they were all filled with the Holy Ghost, and began to speak with other tongues, as the Spirit gave them utterance. Fire fell, an endowment of power and God's presence came to them. In my spirit I see it as a huge rolling ball of fire that flooded and filled every inch of the room and formed a cloud that hovered overhead. Each of them needed an impartation, an infilling of the Holy Spirit, so individual flames separated off. Those individual flames rested upon and took up residence in the believers there that day. The Holy Spirit divided to each man separately as He willed. It was the same Spirit they had seen in Jesus, and whose manifestation had been around them, but now that Spirit was alive within them! It was the promise of Jesus fulfilled.

John 14:16-17 (KJV) *16 And I will pray the Father, and he shall give you another Comforter, that he may abide with you for ever; 17 Even the Spirit of truth; whom the world cannot receive, because it seeth him not, neither knoweth him: <u>but ye know him; for he dwelleth with you, and shall be in you</u>.* They had seen the Holy Spirit at work in Jesus. They had limited, second-hand experience when the Spirit had been with them but He wanted them to know the Holy Spirit. The Holy Ghost moved in to stay with them, to lead and direct and empower them. The plan was to get the glory that Adam lost back into men and the outpouring at Pentecost was the start of it.

John 17:20-23 (KJV) *20 Neither pray I for these alone, but for them also which shall believe on me through their word; 21 That they all* *may be one; as thou, Father, art in me, and I in thee, that they also may be one in us: that the world may believe that thou hast sent me.* We can be in perfect fellowship with God again. *22 And the glory which thou gavest me I have given them; that they may be one, even as we are one: 23 I in them, and thou in me, that they may be made perfect in one; and that the world may know that thou hast sent me, and hast loved them, as thou hast loved me.* Jesus prayed for them to be in perfect union with the Father. He asked that through the power of the blood and the indwelling of the Holy Spirit we would again be clothed in His Glory. He was redeeming not just some but all of what Adam lost. We can walk it out—a life full of the fire and the glory.

You are free to share in the glory because you are washed in the blood. The world should be able to see the results of the blood and the anointing in your life. **Acts 2:38-39 (KJV)** *38 Then Peter said unto them, Repent, and be baptized every one of you in the name of Jesus Christ for the remission of sins, and ye shall receive the gift of the Holy Ghost. 39 For the promise is unto you, and to your children, and to all that are afar off, even as many as the Lord our God shall call.* "The indwelling Spirit communicates to believers all the blessings of the covenant that have been purchased by the Lord Jesus. Apart from Him, the blessing would be beautiful but unobtainable ideas." (Smith p. 252)

When the disciples were at the cross, they saw the blood flow down. They had experiential knowledge that could not be denied. They knew He died; they knew He left an empty grave behind. They had seen him alive after He rose from the dead. They believed in the atonement and the resurrection, and then came Pentecost. They received the anointing to minister it to others. The blood always precedes the fire. They walked in great power and glory because they knew what they had received in the blood. That made them eligible to receive the anointing. They saw the lame walk, lepers cleansed, the blind see at the hands of Jesus. Now they were set free to walk in that same anointing because of the blood. Almost immediately, we see them using the power of the Holy Spirit to heal like Jesus did. **Acts 3:1-8 (KJV)** *1 Now Peter and John went up together into the temple at the hour of prayer, being the ninth hour. 2 And a certain man lame from his mother's womb was carried, whom they laid daily at the gate* *of the temple which is called Beautiful, to ask alms of them that entered into the temple; 3 Who seeing Peter and John about to go into the temple asked an alms. 4 And Peter, fastening his eyes upon him with John, said, Look on us. 5 And he gave heed unto them, expecting to receive something of them. 6 Then Peter said, Silver and gold have I none; but such as I have give I thee: In the name of Jesus Christ of Nazareth rise up and walk. 7 And he took him by the right hand, and lifted him up: and immediately his feet and ankle bones received strength. 8 And he leaping up stood, and walked, and entered with them into the temple, walking, and leaping, and praising God.* Jesus authorized and commissioned them to go and minister in his place. He told them to use the power they had received.

Mark 16:15-20 (KJV) *15 And he said unto them, Go ye into all the world, and preach the gospel to every creature. 16 He that believeth and is baptized shall be saved; but he that believeth not shall be damned. 17 And these signs shall follow them that believe; In my name shall they cast out devils; they shall speak with new tongues; 18 They shall take up serpents; and if they drink any deadly thing, it shall not hurt them; they shall lay hands on the sick, and they shall recover. 19 So then after the Lord had spoken unto them, he was received up into heaven, and sat on the right hand of God. 20 And they went forth, and preached every where, the Lord working with them, and confirming the word with signs following. Amen.*

The blood fell; the power of the Holy Spirit filled believers, and they did the works that He called them to do. It is the same power at work in believers today.

Romans 5:1 - 2 (KJV) *1 Therefore being justified by faith, we have peace with God through our Lord Jesus Christ: 2 By whom also we have access by faith into this grace wherein we stand, and rejoice in hope of the glory of God.*

She Put The Blood First A Testimony Of The Miraculous

Acts 1:8 (KJV) *8 But ye shall receive power, after that the Holy Ghost is come upon you: and ye shall be witnesses unto me both in Jerusalem, and in all Judaea, and in Samaria, and unto the uttermost part of the earth.* The Lord spoke to those early believers to go and share what had happened to them. He was saying tell everyone. He wanted them to start at home and work their way into areas they never thought they would go. I have tried to fulfill that calling. Becky is one person God sent me to. It was He, not I, who did the work. The glory of the LORD was seen because God loves us. God sent Jesus who shed blood which brought a powerful manifestation 2000 years later in Becky's heart and body.

Becky was living across the street from me when she was diagnosed with MS [Multiple Sclerosis]. My neighbor, Janet, and I both prayed for her all the time. I did not really know her, but one day I felt led to talk to her about healing. She was courteous and even curious, but she said she was not all that interested. Over the next few weeks we became friends. We talked about healing and about salvation. We even talked about the second coming of Christ.

Multiple Sclerosis had ravaged her body. She could no longer work. She had really limited ability to walk and she fatigued easily. Her right eye had tunnel vision. Her right hand would shake if she tried to lift anything and she had limited grip strength in both hands. There was weakness in both legs, but her right leg was the most severely affected. She could drag it, but the muscles had begun to atrophy and so her foot turned inward. I did therapy with her at home and it took both my hands and all my strength to turn her foot even an inch. I could not turn it completely back into place. As our friendship grew, I urged her to come to church with me. I told her that she could be totally healed. I pretty much promised her a miracle. Finally she agreed to go to church with me.

The first night she went to church, we sat near the back of the church because she just could not walk much farther. During altar call, she stood up and began struggling down the aisle. I did not help her because I knew it was something she needed to do herself. After dragging herself about 12 feet, she literally fell into the pastor's arms. She said, "I need healing so bad, but I need Jesus more." She got saved that night. She got the blood to work in her life. She was less concerned about the physical needs in her body, because her heart was so hungry for more of God. That is vital—always put relationship with Him first and He will see to your needs. **Psalm 37:4 (KJV)** *4 Delight thyself also in the LORD; and he shall give thee the desires of thine heart.*

Her heart and spirit were more important than her physical healing. It was about a week later that she asked to be filled with the Holy Spirit. As soon as she had received the Holy Spirit she told her live-in boyfriend to move out. She decided to live holy, but she still loved him. We prayed earnestly for him to turn his life over to Christ, which he did. As soon as he got saved, Paul asked her to marry him. Our pastor called the church to fast, stating that he expected a miracle. Becky never knew that we were fasting for her.

THERE IS FIRE IN THE BLOOD

Our Pastor was a strong believer in the power of God, and he knew this teaching from the Lord. **Matthew 17:14-21 (KJV)** *14 And when they were come to the multitude, there came to him a certain man, kneeling down to him, and saying, 15 Lord, have mercy on my son: for he is lunatick, and sore vexed: for ofttimes he falleth into the fire, and oft into the water. 16 And I brought him to thy disciples, and they could not cure him. 17 Then Jesus answered and said, O faithless and perverse generation, how long shall I be with you? how long shall I suffer you? bring him hither to me. 18 And Jesus rebuked the devil; and he departed out of him: and the child was cured from that very hour. 19 Then came the disciples to Jesus apart, and said, Why could not we cast him out? 20 And Jesus said unto them, Because of your unbelief: for verily I say unto you, If ye have faith as a grain of mustard seed, ye shall say unto this mountain, Remove hence to yonder place; and it shall remove; and nothing shall be impossible unto you. 21 Howbeit this kind goeth not out but by prayer and fasting.* Fasting does not change God; it does nothing in the natural world either. Believers are changed when we fast. Fasting makes us more sensitive to the Holy Spirit and lifts our expectations. The church was about to make a demand on the anointing, and so as a body we chose to fast, banning unbelief from our hearts.

Two nights before their wedding God miraculously healed Becky. The pastor called her to come forward, and because she could not stand for long, he had her sit in a chair. He prayed and Janet and I lay hands on her legs. **Mark 16:18 (KJV)** *...they shall lay hands on the sick, and they shall recover.* He said, "In the name of Jesus, be healed" and that foot just snapped into place. Disease bowed its knee before the Almighty. It was amazing. She did not just show improvement; it was a total miracle. She could run, jump, sit on the floor and lift her legs and then stand right back up without using her hands to push off. She got the whole thing in one night. I think the reason she got such incredible results was that she put things in the proper order. She did it the right way—God's way. She got under the blood, let the Lord teach her a little and then the fire of the Holy Ghost took care of all her other needs. Three weeks after she got saved, she walked down the aisle of the church to get married in high heels. It has been over thirty-five years and Becky is still healed. God is faithful to those who seek him with their whole hearts.

Ephesians 2:13 (KJV) *13 But now in Christ Jesus ye who sometimes were far off are made nigh by the blood of Christ.*

The Blood Is Enough

At every crime scene, the most compelling evidence is blood evidence. Crime Scene Investigators (CSI's) can follow a blood trail to reveal more evidence, a weapon, a body or a witness. They dig behind floor boards and light switches and under carpet to find a hidden drop of blood to connect an individual with what happened at the crime scene. They can find blood that appeared to have been cleaned away in the wildest places. They locate hidden blood using luminal in wristwatches, and under the diamonds in wedding rings. The blood testifies that this person was there when the blood was shed. **It all comes down to the blood. Is it on you or not?**

Hebrews 12:22-24 (KJV) *22 But ye are come unto mount Sion, and unto the city of the living God, the heavenly Jerusalem, and to an innumerable company of angels, 23 To the general assembly and church of the firstborn, which are written in heaven, and to God the Judge of all, and to the spirits of just men made perfect, 24 And to Jesus the mediator of the new covenant, and to the blood of sprinkling, that speaketh better things than that of Abel.*

The blood of Abel's sacrifice spoke of his justification by faith and his acceptance and then later his own lifeblood cried out for vengeance, but the blood of Jesus cries out for our freedom and our deliverance. It declares our innocence. **Hebrews 12:24 (TMSG)** *24 You've come to Jesus, who presents us with a new covenant, a fresh charter from God. He is the Mediator of this covenant. The murder of Jesus, unlike Abel's—a homicide that cried out for vengeance—became a proclamation of grace.* **Is there blood on you?**

Jesus came to earth to truly identify with man, and man comes to salvation so that we can identify with God. **Hebrews 4:15 (KJV)** *15 For we have not an high priest which cannot be touched with the feeling of our infirmities; but was in all points tempted like as we are, yet without sin.* God wants us to know how much we are loved and valued and that He would go to extreme measures to bring us into fellowship with him again. Through Jesus mankind got back everything that Adam lost. But he did not just want us free from sin and able to fellowship with him He wanted us to be powerful and mighty and to use our oneness with him to change the world.

Revelation 1:5-6 (KJV) *5 And from Jesus Christ, who is the faithful witness, and the first begotten of the dead, and the prince of the kings of the earth. Unto him that loved us, and washed us from our sins in his own blood, 6 And hath made us kings and priests unto God and his Father; to him be glory and dominion for ever and ever. Amen.* Jesus was the first to come back from the grave demonstrating victory over death, but He gave that same victory to us. **Galatians 2:20 (KJV)** *I am crucified with Christ nevertheless I live; yet not I, but Christ liveth in me; and the life which I now live in the flesh I live by the faith of the Son of God, who loved me, and gave himself for me.* Because He lives—we live. We have nothing to fear because we are washed clean.

Yesterday when Donna and I were talking about standing before God in heaven, she said something about how she still fails, still sins, how she "doesn't do enough" and that she knew that those things were on the books against her and I said, **"The blood is enough."** Because whatever we do, wherever we have failed and sinned the blood of Jesus covers it and makes us acceptable. <u>That blood is more than enough. We do not earn anything and whatever acts of service we do, is a response to the blood not an addition.</u> We know the blood is enough to change the heart, to heal the body, to set free the ones in bondage. The blood is enough if the blood is applied. Make much of the blood and never forget what was done for you. It is not the blood and your good works. Any time we try to attach anything else to the blood we make it seem less effective. It is never the blood plus—it is the blood period. It is all about what He did and your faith in it.

A few years ago, I attended a conference where Gracia Burnham spoke. She was a missionary in the Philippines and was kidnapped by Muslim extremists in May of 2001. The guerrilla group took her and her husband along with 18 other hostages. They sent out demands for ransom. Over time some were released and some were killed. The United States does not negotiate with terrorists and so no ransom was sent from our government. She was held for over a year, and the guerrillas had her make video pleas for money. She became so ill that her friends and missionary supporters were fearful she would die even if she was not killed by her captors.

She said they were greatly relieved to find out that people who were concerned for their safety had accumulated a substantial sum and sent it to pay for their ransom. When it arrived they expected to go free, but instead the guerrillas said, "It is not enough." They demanded a second installment. She knew that was impossible; she was devastated. Her husband comforted her with the fact that when Jesus stood before the whole of the spirit world and held out his blood as a ransom it was accepted—the blood was enough.

Remember what is says in **Revelation 12:11 (KJV)** *11 And they overcame him by the blood of the Lamb, and by the word of their testimony; and they loved not their lives unto the death.* Billye Brim said, "We need to possess all the secrets revealed in the Word pertaining to the power availed us. The Word of God is a blood covenant. Every provision and promise is ratified by the blood of Jesus...there must be a personal application of the blood of Christ in order to stem the tide of spiritual destruction in the life of the child of God." [Brim p. 121.] Just like Moses had them apply the blood of a lamb to their doorposts to keep the destroyer out, so you must apply the blood in your life to protect your spirit, your mind, your body, and all that pertains to you. There was blood shed and it is on you at your request. The blood of Jesus represents his life given for you, and imparted to you. When Christ shed his blood at Calvary, He gave us his life. When we call upon the Lord to wash us and cover us with his blood, we will experience his life giving power. Each provision in the covenant and every promise of God was permanently sealed by the blood of Jesus. Call upon that blood, plead that blood over the circumstance and hold it against all that opposes you. No enemy can withstand the Blood of Jesus.

Revelation 12:11 (KJV) *11 And they overcame him by the blood of the Lamb, and by the word of their testimony; and they loved not their lives unto the death.* His death produces salvation. They overcame by holding to the covenant relationship they had, identifying themselves with the death and resurrection of the Lord.

The blood is symbolic of all He bought for us. We were blood washed. Salvation is in that blood and deliverance and healing are in the blood too. The blood is enough to make us overcomers. It is his life in us. There is cleansing and an awareness of relationship in it. We depend fully on the One who bought us with his blood. We must plead the blood, make much of the blood. The life is in the blood—his life is in us because of that blood.

They also used *"Word of their testimony."* It matters what you say about the Lord and your situation and the scriptures. **Proverbs 18:21 (KJV)** 21 *Death and life are in the power of the tongue: and they that love it shall eat the fruit thereof.* Your words either bring victory or defeat. As we spend more time with him, and read the scriptures, that word becomes rooted in us. We become strong believers, overcomers by virtue of our relationship with him. Overcomers speak what they believe, and stand upon the Word of God.

Revelation 12:12 (KJV) 12 ... Woe to the inhabiters of the earth and of the sea! for the devil is come down unto you, having great wrath, because he knoweth that he hath but a short time. The devil is on a rampage trying to steal and kill and destroy. He is angry because his days are short.

THERE IS FIRE IN THE BLOOD

There is very little time to do damage to the kingdom of God and ruin the testimony of believers and stop the spread of the Gospel. He is desperate and venomous, spewing his poison everywhere he can. He would use your mouth to speak of death and destruction and depravation. He would use you to criticize and condemn and stop the power of the blood from flowing if he could, but you can stop him. Never say anything that denies the power of the blood in your life. Speak what the scriptures say. Regardless of what the world says, trust in Jesus. If the doctor says you have cancer and it is incurable and you will die, those are just facts. Jesus is the Way, the Truth and the Life. He says, *"By my stripes you were healed, you shall live and not die, I will make a way where there seems to be no way."* The One who is truth is much stronger than any fact—always agree with Truth.

Matthew 12:34-35 (KJV) ... *for out of the abundance of the heart the mouth speaketh. 35 A good man out of the good treasure of the heart bringeth forth good things: and an evil man out of the evil treasure bringeth forth evil things. So what we declare on an ongoing basis is what we really believe. Since that is true, as a born again believers, we speak in agreement with the scriptures. We can face the world with confidence. It is his blood that saved us, cleansed us, covered us, protects us and lets us stand in His glory.* **The blood is enough. It is our way into his presence, into the glory—into the Fire!**

The devil has tried to rob the church of the truth about the blood. He does not want us to use it in practical ways. He wants us to ignore the blood, so we will be sick and broken, weak and distressed, faithless and easy to kill off. "Surrender yourself to God the Holy Spirit. Fix the eyes of your heart on the blood. Open your whole inner being to its power." (Murray p. 40) By virtue of the blood we are now his righteous representatives on earth. We are here to present him afresh to the world. We want everyone to see him in us. If we will cling to his blood then we can display his nature and his character and his power. God wants us to live free, full of the fire of his Holy Spirit. He was willing to shed blood to get it done.

If the heavenly CSI team investigated you thoroughly would they find evidence of the blood of Jesus? <u>His blood on us proves we are</u>

<u>not guilty and worthy of death.</u> We are identified with the one who died. His blood on me means I am in the covenant. If we want fire in our hearts, we know how to find it. **There is fire in the blood.**

Works Cited

Billye Brim, *The Blood and the Glory*, (Tulsa, OK: Harrison House, 1995), p. 41, 42, 43, 50, 121.

Andrew Murray, T*he Power of the Blood of Jesus*, (New Kensington, PA: Whitaker House, 1993), p. 9, 11, 14, 15, 17, 27, 28, 29, 40.

Malcolm Smith, *The Lost Secret of the New Covenant*, (Tulsa, OK: Harrison House, 2002), p. 12, 13, 27, 31, 50, 77, 101, 102, 106, 138, 252.

Charles Spurgeon, P*ower in the Blood*, (New Kensington, PA: Whitaker House, 1996), p. 23, 43, 44, 45, 46.

James Strong, *Strong's Exhaustive Concordance of the Bible*, (Nashville, TN: Royal Publisher, Inc., 1979)

Maxwell Whyte, *The Power of the Blood*, (New Kensington, PA: Whitaker House, 1973), p.14, 17, 24.

Scripture References are from the King James Version of the Bible and The Message Bible

THERE IS FIRE IN THE BLOOD

www.ingramcontent.com/pod-product-compliance
Lightning Source LLC
Chambersburg PA
CBHW071534080526
44588CB00011B/1664